MAKING SENSE OF THE FINANCIAL STATEMENTS
Understanding, Analysis, and Interpretation

Godwin Akasie

AmberBooks • •

First published 2012
By Dothouse Consulting, London, England

Text © 2011 Godwin Akasie

The right of Godwin Akasie to be identified as author of this work has been asserted by him in accordance with the Copyright, Design and Patents Act 1988.

Printed and bound in the U.S.A
Createspace™
An Amazon.com Company

All rights reserved. No part of this book may be reproduced, transmitted or stored in an information retrieval system in any form or by any means, graphic, electronic, or mechanical, including photocopying, taping and recording, without prior written permission from the publisher.

The Author

Godwin Akasie is the author of the self-development booklet: *Thoughts on Self-Improvement* (Principles, Timeless Quotations, Statements and Tit-bits from the Sages and Enlightenment Thinkers, Past & Present). He also wrote the *Echoes from the Present Past*, and *Accounting Essentials* – Concepts, Terms and Meaning. Other titles by the author include: *Shadows and Colours, Holding On, Painted Walls* - Prose and Verses, and *The GreenPath Orison* (A collection of Suggestions and Personal Affirmations).

He had worked in both private and public sectors, rising from the ranks to the top level of management, preparing financial budgets and periodic statements, reviewing operations and activities, analyzing and interpreting accounting results, appraising the strengths of risk management and internal controls, monitoring compliance issues, and evaluating designs of new information systems and major modifications to existing systems, and advising on optimal use of company resources.

He left the University of Benin as an Accountant and resigned from his position as the Assistant Chief /Project Accountant of the then Bendel State Public Utilities Board, Benin City, to pioneer and set up the Accounts Department of Great Merchant Bank Ltd in Lagos in the early eighties. He is a Past President of the Mortgage Bankers Association of Nigeria and left the banking industry as the Head of Internal Controls and Chief Inspector of Liberty Bank PLC to establish his accounting practice, *Akasie Godwin Onyemaechi & Co* (Chartered Accountants).

A Fellow of the Institute of Chartered Accountants of Nigeria (FCA) and a holder of a Bachelor's Degree in Accountancy and Master's Degree in Business Administration (MBA) from the University of Nigeria and University of Benin respectively, Mr. Akasie is a widely travelled personality. He now lives in London though he still finds time to regularly return to walk the coastlines of the Lagos lagoons, where he was first captured by the wonders and symmetry of nature that inspires much of his thinking and writing.

He is passionate about teaching and facilitating in business training courses and he had taught accounting for many years at the extramural department of the University of Benin, COSIT programme, University of Lagos, as well as in private business schools in Lagos and Benin City where he helped to develop and write the accounting courses.

CONTENTS

		page
i. Introduction		i-iii

Part 1: Summary of related Accounting Concepts, Terms, Principles, Standards and Phrases ... 1

1.1.	Account	1
1.2.	Accounts	1
1.3.	Accounting	1
1.4.	Accounting Classification	1
1.5.	Accounts classes	2
1.6.	Accountant	3
1.7.	Accounting Cost	3
1.8.	Accounting Period	3
1.9.	Accounting Profit or Loss	4
1.10.	Accounting Standards and Frameworks	4
1.11.	Accounting Concepts	7
1.12.	Accounting Convention	7
1.13.	Accrual Concept	7
1.14.	Accounting Ratio	7
1.15.	Activity/Cost Drivers	8
1.16.	Accounting Entity Assumption	8
1.17.	Accounting Entity	8
1.18.	Accounting Software	8
1.19.	Accounting System	8
1.20.	Cash	8
1.21.	Cash Accounting	9
1.22.	Cash and Cash Equivalents	9
1.23.	Cash Dividend	9
1.24.	Cash Earnings	9
1.25.	Cash Flow	9
1.26.	Cash Flow Analysis	9
1.27.	Cash Flow Cycle	9
1.28.	Cash Flow Forecast	9
1.29.	Cash Flow Forecast Statement	10
1.30.	Cash at Bank	10
1.31.	Cash Flows	10
1.32.	Cash on Hand	10
1.33.	Cash out flows	10
1.34.	Cash Operating Cycle	10
1.35.	Cash Reserve Ratio	10
1.36.	Cash Shortage and Overage	10

1.37.	Financial Restructuring	11
1.38.	Financial Reporting	11
1.39.	International Financial Reporting Standards	11
1.40.	Investment	11
1.41.	Investment Appraisal/Valuation	12
1.42.	Investment Banker	12
1.43.	Investment Centre	12
1.44.	Investment Goods	12
1.45.	Investment Manager	12
1.46.	Investment Property	12
1.47.	Public Versus Management Financials	12
1.48.	Reconciling Differences between Accounting standards/Frameworks	13
1.49.	The Reason to Note the different Accounting Standards	13

Part 2: Financial Reporting Frameworks with Summarised Guidance on the Preparation of Financial Statements – IFRS for SMEs — 14

2.1. Why IFRS for SMEs	14
2.2. Scope of IFRS for SMEs	15
2.3. Requirement of Historical Cost Accounting	16
2.4. Concepts	16
2.5. Presentation	16
2.6. First-time Adoption	16
2.7. Selection of Accounting Policies	17
2.8. Financial Statements	17
2.8.1. What they are	17
2.8.2. Objectives of Financial Statements	18
2.8.3. Financial Decisions	18
2.8.4. Users of Financial Statements and Accounting Information	18
2.8.5. Uses of Accounting Information	18
2.8.6. Responsibility for Financial Statements	19
2.8.7. Qualitative Characteristics Financial Statements	
2.9. Financial Statement Analysis	19
2.10. Statement of Financial Position (Balance Sheet)	19
2.11. Statement of Comprehensive Income and Expenses	21
2.11.1. Income Statement	21
2.11.2. Statement of Recognised Income and Expenses	21
2.11.3. Elements of the Statement of Comprehensive Income and Expenses	21
2.12. Material, Extra-ordinary, and Exceptional Items	22
2.13. Statement of Changes in Equity	23

2.14. Statement of Income and Retained Earnings	23
2.15. Statement of Cash Flows	24
2.16. Notes and Supplementary Schedules to the Financial Statements	24
2.17. Accounting Policies, Estimates and Errors	25
2.18. Critical Accounting Estimates and Judgements	25
2.19. Correction of Prior-period Errors	26
2.20. Related Parties	26
2.21. Events after the End of the Reporting Period	27
2.22. Balance Sheet Elements – Assets and Liabilities	26
2.23. Fair Value	33
2.24. Impairment of Financial Instruments measured at cost or amortised at cost	33
2.25. De-recognition of Financial Assets	33
2.26. De-recognition of Financial Liabilities	34
2.27. Further Issues relating to Financial Instruments	34
2.28. Hedge Accounting	34
2.29. Impairment of non-Financial Assets	35
2.30. Provisions and Contingencies	36
2.31. Employee Benefits	37
2.32. Income Taxes	39
2.33. Leases	40
2.34. Business Combinations, Consolidated Financial Statements, and Investments in Associates and Joint Ventures	41
2.35. Liabilities and Equity	45
2.36. Income and Expenses	46
2.37. Currencies	48
2.38. Hyperinflation	49
2.39. Special Activities	50
2.40. A Standard Format for Balance Sheet Preparation under IFRS (IAS1)	51
2.41. Balance Sheet Elements	52
2.42. Income Statements	52
2.43. An Example of Income Statement presentation	55
2.44. Drivers of Cost and Revenue	56
2.45. Analysing the Key Financial Statements	56
Part 3: Financial/Accounting Ratios, Analysis and Interpretation	**57**
3.1. Horizontal Analysis	57
3.2. An Illustration	57
3.3. Financial Ratio Analysis	59
3.4. An Illustrative Example	60

3.5. Accounting Ratios	62
3.6. Principal Accounting Ratios	62
3.7. Financial Profitability and Asset Turnover Ratios – Calculations	64
3.8. Financial Stability Ratios – Calculations	75
3.9. Financial Investment Ratios – Calculations	81
3.10. Working Capital Cycle, Ratios and Considerations	88
3.11. Limitations of Financial Ratios	89
3.12. Trend Analysis	91
3.13. Time Series	91

Part 4: Reading and Interpreting Financial Statements — 93

4.1. Reading and Interpreting Financial Statements	93
4.2. Worked Examples – Questions 1 – 17	93-130

Part 5: Cash Flow Statements — 134

5.1. Purpose of Cash flow Statements	134
5.2. An Illustration of a Cash Flow Statement	136
5.3. Components of the Cash Flows	139
5.3.1. Operating Activities	139
5.3.2. Determination of Cash Flow from Operating Activities	142
5.3.3. Direct/Indirect Methods of determining cash flows	142
5.3.4. Determining Cash flow from Operating Activities using Direct/Indirect Methods	143
5.3.5. Cash Flows from Investments and Finance Servicing	146
5.3.6. Determining Cash Flow from Finance Servicing	147
5.3.7. Cash Flows from Capital Expenditure and Financial Investments	148
5.3.8. Cash Flows from Acquisitions and Disposals	148
5.3.9. Cash Flows from Equity Dividends	149
5.3.10. Cash Flows from Liquid Resources	149
5.3.11. Financing Cash Flows	150
5.3.12. Determining the Cash Flows from Financing Activities	150
5.3.13. Requirements of the IFRS on reconciling the movement of cash	151
5.3.14. Reconciliation of Net Cash Flow to Movement in Net Debt	152
5.3.15. Areas to Note	154
5.3.16. Determination of Cash Flows from a set of Data	155
5.3.17. "Small" Companies Exempted from the provisions of the FRS1	156

5.3.18. Advantages of the Cash Flow Statements	157
5.3.19. Limitations of Cash Flow Statements	157
5.3.20. Definition of Cash under the FRS	158
5.3.21. Cash-based Accounting Ratios	159
5.3.22. Linkages between the Financial Statements	160
5.3.23. Interpreting Cash Flow Data	160
5.3.24. Unbalanced Financial Development	161
5.3.25. Over-Capitalisation	162
5.3.26. Over-Trading	162

Part 6: Practice Questions and Answers on Cash Flow Statements — 163

Questions 1 – 6 — 163-182

Part 7: IFRS for SMEs – An Illustrative Example of a set of Consolidated Financial Statements — 189

INTRODUCTION

Established business entities show their stewardship - the report card of trading activities - to the stakeholders through the production of periodic financial statements. This takes the form of either general or specific purpose financial statements.

The general purpose financial statements are published for external users including owners who are not involved in managing the business, existing and potential creditors, and credit rating agencies, and they include those statements that are presented separately or within another public document such as an annual report. The objective of general purpose financial statements prepared in accordance with the IFRS for SMEs is to "provide useful information about an entity's financial position, performance and cash flows to a wide range of users who are not in a position to demand reports tailored to meet their particular information needs. Accordingly, general purpose financial statements are directed towards the common information needs of a wide range of users, such as, shareholders, creditors and employees."

The IFRS for SMEs is designed to apply to the general purpose financial statements and other financial reporting of those profit-oriented entities that do not have public accountability.

A typical example of general purpose financial statements is where an entity that does not have public accountability voluntarily prepares its financial statements in compliance with the requirements of the IFRS for SMEs. The entity sends the financial statements to the entity's primary suppliers, bankers and non-manager owners. The entity makes an explicit and unreserved statement of compliance with the IFRS for SMEs in the notes. In this case, the entity's financial statements are general purpose financial statements — prepared on the basis (the IFRS for SMEs) that is designed to provide useful information to a wide range of users who are not in a position to demand reports tailored to meet their particular information needs.

Sometimes, companies produce financial statements only for a specific purpose — for the use of owner-managers, or for tax reporting or other non-securities regulatory filing purposes. The financial statements produced solely for those purposes are not necessarily general purpose financial statements.

An example is where an entity that does not have public accountability prepares financial statements in compliance with the tax requirements for calculating taxable income (and tax expenses) in the country in which it operates. The country's tax requirements are different from the requirements of the IFRS for SMEs. The entity sends the financial statements only to the tax authorities. The entity makes an explicit and unreserved statement of compliance with local tax requirements in the notes. Here, the entity's financial statements are special purpose financial statements—they are produced specifically for tax reporting (i.e. tax accounts). The requirements of tax accounts are determined by fiscal considerations and are unlikely to be designed to provide useful information to a wide range of users who are not in a position to demand reports tailored to meet their particular information needs. Accordingly, the tax accounts are unlikely to be general purpose financial statements.
There are thus different types of financial statements. The nature and degree of the differences between them is determined on the basis of users' needs and cost-benefit analyses.

In practice, the benefits of applying accounting standards differ across reporting entities, depending primarily on the nature, number and information needs of the users of their financial statements. The related costs may not differ significantly. But they must lend themselves to the understanding and proper interpretation of the users. Hence the application of generally accepted accounting standards, processes, procedures and principles in the presentation of readily understandable, reliable, relevant and comparable financial statements.

Adopting the International Financial Reporting Standards (IFRS) has added benefits for the users through the comparability and transparency provided by a consistent application of a set of world-wide financial reporting standards. Understanding these standards and background requirements is important to the appreciation of the contents and purpose of financial statements.

The objectives of this book are four folds:
1. To help individuals obtain skillful insights on industry dynamics and company performance (for SMEs in particular) from publicly available financial statements.
2. To further progress the financial analysis and interpretation skills of users of financial accounting statements – especially the financial and investment decision makers.

3. To assist understanding of why financial skills are important for business strategic decision making.
4. To help improve the understanding of language style and terms as used by practitioners in the production of financial statements.

Seven topical areas are covered to underscore the understanding, analysis and interpretation of financial statements.

- **Part 1** deals with a summary of related background Accounting Concepts, Terms, Principles, Standards and Phrases. The information enables the reader to appreciate the language of the accountant as used in the preparation of the financial statements.
- **Part 2** summaries the Financial Reporting Frameworks and provides guidance on the preparation of financial statements – with emphasis on the IFRS for SMEs. It helps the reader with the background details back of the elements of the financial statements. This part also gives studied details on the basic Financial Statements – Balance Sheet, Income Statement, and Cash Flow Statement and how these relate to each other. Understanding of these statements, their contents that is, enables one to readily gain the knowledge of the operating activities of the reporting entity.
- **Part 3** deals with the common Financial Ratios, what they stand for and how they are calculated and used in gaining insight into the performance of the reporting entity. The information enables you to more confidently and effectively interpret financial and statistical data in the financial presentations and to provide convincing arguments to support your observations and recommendations.
- **Part 4** covers the Reading and Interpretation of financial statements, worked examples – questions and suggested answers - putting into practice the understanding garnered from the preceding parts.
- **In Part 5** is detailed the Cash flow statement presentations, while **Part 6** deals with Practice Questions and suggested Answers.
- Finally, in the appendix, **Part 7** is an illustrative example of a set of Consolidated Financial Statements prepared under the requirements of the IFRS for SMEs, the purpose of which is to highlight the standard format for financial statements preparation.

This book arms you with the analytical skills designed to improve your understanding and interpretation of financial statements. Once you master the details of the message, your overall analytical skills rises and your ability to read and communicate accounting data becomes more effective as a direct result.

Godwin Akasie

Part 1
Summary of Related Accounting Concepts, Terms, Principles, Standards and Phrases

1.1 Account - This term is used to refer to a section of the General Ledger, i.e. a ledger record; it is a summarised form of all transactions that have taken place with the particular entity or value specified (e.g. Billy's Account, Property, Plant & Equipment Account, Rent Account, Electricity Account, Salaries and Wages Account etc).

1.2 Accounts – This is used to refer to the financial records of the transactions of a business entity.

1.3 Accounting – This term may refer to:
(a) A subject of study, an all-embracing term covering many areas of disciplines including auditing, taxation, financial statement analysis; and
(b) The process of collecting, recording, measuring, interpreting, and communicating financial information to the users about the reporting entity.

1.4 Accounting Classification - A usual classification of the subject of "Accounting" is into what is called "Financial Accounting," and "Cost and Management Accounting". When this classification is used, financial accounting is considered as being restricted to the provision of accounting information for external user groups (external reporting), while Cost and Management accounting, on the other hand, are used to describe the provision of information for management (internal reporting). However, this definition of financial accounting is too narrow. Financial accounting therefore is more generally defined as "consisting of statements prepared to summarise the overall financial progress and position of an entity (using historical data and constrained by any regulatory requirements), whether prepared for managers, owners, creditors or any other interested party. It reports to interested parties the results of the decisions taken by management. Cost Accounting is the establishment of budgets, standard costs and actual costs of operations, processes, activities or products, and the analysis of variances, profitability or social use of funds. Management Accounting is the process of identification, measurement, accumulation, analysis, preparation, interpretation and communication of information used by management to plan, evaluate, and control the activities of a business entity. It is concerned with day-to-day planning, control, and decision making. It is not covered by any regulatory requirements.

1.5 Accounts Classes – Basically, there are two classes of accounts, namely: Personal Accounts, and Impersonal Accounts.

•**Personal Accounts** - These are the accounts that deal with persons – Creditors and Debtors. Such persons include individuals, companies, corporations, Agencies, etc. In Personal Accounts, debit entries are made for value received or expenses incurred, while credit entries show the value given out or gains earned. Personal accounts can also refer to the capital accounts of each of the partners of a firm and each shareholder of a company where financial transactions relating to the individual are recorded.

• **Impersonal Accounts** - These accounts fall into two sub-categories – Real Accounts and Nominal Accounts.

• **Real Accounts** - Are the accounts that deal with tangible assets, such as plant and machinery, furniture and fittings, motor vehicles, etc. Here, debit entries are made when assets are bought, while credit entries are made when assets are sold or disposed of.

• **Nominal Accounts** – This class of accounts deals with gains, income, expenses, and losses, e.g. discounts, commissions, dividends, rents, salaries and wages, etc. Debit entries are made for expenses and losses; while credit entries are made for gains and incomes.

However, some impersonal accounts are really personal in importance. For example, Capital Account and Drawings Account are personal accounts either of the proprietor of the business or of the partners who are creditors to the business to the extent of the value of their capitals and debtors to the extent of the value of their drawings.

Some accounts are both real and nominal. For instance, the Sales Account is a Real Account as far as the goods themselves are concerned, but nominal as relates to the gain or loss arising from the sales.

Debit balances in the ledger accounts could represent assets, expenses, or losses; and credit balances may be liabilities or gains.

Classes of Ledger Accounts and Nature of Balances

	Name of Account	Nature Or Types	Examples	Debit Entries	Credit Entries	Debit Balances	Credit Balances	Treatment In the Final Accounts
1	Personal	Persons	Debtors Creditors Capital	Values received or Expenses incurred	Values given out or Gains earned	Amount due business from persons	Amount due persons from Business	Balance Sheet
2	Impersonal: Real	Assets	Plant, Machinery, Premises, Furniture & Fittings	Values coming in	Values going out	Assets to the Business	Does not normally exist	Balance Sheet
3	Impersonal: Nominal	Expenses or Gains	Salaries and Wages, Rent, Discounts, Commissions, etc	Expenses	Gains or Profits	Expenses over a period	Gains or profits over a period	Profit and Loss Account

1.6 Accountant – An Accountant is a person who performs accounting services; he/she maintains the business records of an entity - a person or an organisation. Accountants prepare financial statements and tax returns, audit financial records, and develop financial plans. They work in private accounting (e.g., for a company), public accounting (e.g., for a professional firm), not-for-profit accounting (e.g., for a governmental agency and charities and clubs). Accountants often specialise in a particular area such as taxes, cost accounting, auditing, and management advisory services. A book-keeper is normally distinguished from an accountant as one who employs lesser professional skills. The book-keeping function is primarily one of recording transactions in the journal and posting to the ledger.

1.7 Accounting Cost – Is the monetary value of an economic resource used up in the production of goods or delivering of services.

1.8 Accounting period - This refers to any period for which a company prepares its accounts and it is usually 12 months.
The first accounting period does not start until a company starts to trade,

or when its profits first become liable to corporation tax. The end of accounting period is earliest of: 12 months after the start of period, end of company's period of accounts, and date the company ceases to trade. And corporation tax is based on profits made during an accounting period.

1.9 Accounting Profit or Loss – This is the difference between the total incomes and the total explicit costs. It is the profit or loss for the accounting period under review using certain types of income and expenditure items that are allowed.

1.10 Accounting Standards and Frameworks - Companies' financial statements are based on one of a number of accounting standards or frameworks. These include principles, bases, concepts and conventions. These frameworks form the basis by which a business entity prepares its financial statements and by which auditors express their opinion.

The focus of the Accounting Standards is to assist companies to produce financial statements that users can:

- Rely on for their accuracy and consistency – i.e. the **"true and fair view"** concept.
- Compare with over time i.e. in trend analysis; and
- Compare with those of another or more different companies.

- **Standards** are principles-based, directing attention to the outcome achieved by reporting, the legal requirements of which are set out in the Companies Act.
- They provide key assumptions that the company will continue to operate indefinitely (Going Concern), and that events are recognised when they occur, not as cash is received or paid (Accrual basis).
- Standards make for flexibility in reporting, providing framework for company's accounting policies which can be tailored according to the needs of each company.
- The Standards frequency for financial statement publication is annually; though listed companies may also report quarterly (although these may not be audited).
- In the Standards, companies are only permitted to change policies with "good reason;" and the reasons and implications of such changes must be clearly stated in the report.

(i) **Accounting Bases** – These are the methods developed for expressing or applying fundamental accounting concepts to the financial transactions and items of a business entity.

By their nature, the accounting bases are more diverse and numerous than the fundamental concepts, since they evolve in response to the variety and complexity of types of business and business transactions, and for this reason they may justifiably exist more than one recognised accounting basis for dealing with particular items, e.g. stock valuation, provision for depreciation, accounting for leases and hire purchase contracts. All these have different bases of accounting for them. As an example, for depreciation, the straight-line method or the Reducing Balance method could be used.

(ii) **Accounting Policies** - Are the specific accounting bases, principles, conventions, rules and practices judged by the business entity to be most appropriate to their circumstances and adopted by them for the purpose of preparing their financial statements i.e. for reflecting transactions and other activities in the financial statements. Policies must be consistent with accounting standards and provisions of the Companies Act with the aim of giving a true and fair view and must be assessed against the objectives of relevance, reliability, comparability and understandability. The two most important concepts that affect the selection of accounting policies are the going concern and accrual concepts. Business entities are required to prepare financial statements on the basis of going concern and accrual concepts, except for cash flow information and/or if the entity is in the process of liquidation.

(iii) **Accounting Principles** – These are the rules and guidelines of accounting. They determine such matters as the measurement of assets, the timing of revenue recognition, and the accrual of expenses. The "ground rules" for financial reporting are referred to as Generally Accepted Accounting Principle(s) – GAAP. The GAAP contains the framework of guidelines that covers financial accounting, including the standards, conventions, and rules that are followed. The UK Companies Act, for example, recognises the four fundamental accounting concepts of going concern, accruals, prudence and consistency as Accounting Principles.

The other principle is the requirement of a business entity in deciding the aggregate value of any item to be included in the financial statement, to first separately determine the value of the individual asset or liability under consideration.

For instance, when stock is valued at the lower of cost and net realisable value, the amount must first be calculated for the separate types of stock and then added together. The sixth principle as recognised by the Companies Act is the principle of "Substance over form" which requires a business entity, in deciding how values are reflected in the financial statements, to have regard to the economic substance (rather than only the legal form) of the transaction or arrangement under consideration.

(iv) Other principles or conventions include:

(a) **Entity or Accounting Unit Convention** - For accounting purposes, the business is a different entity, separate from the proprietors or owners with different accounts kept for its transactions.

(b) **Accounting Period Convention** – For accounting purposes, the lifespan of the business entity is arbitrarily divided into fixed periods of time referred to as the accounting period, normally one year in interval, at the end of which financial statements are prepared to reflect the transactions that occurred.

(c) **Materiality Convention** - In accounting, financial statements are to consider the relative importance (materiality) of each item as an individual or collectively as a group in the overall context of the financial statements. As an example, an expense of CU2, 000 could be material to an entity making a profit of CU6, 000 per annum but it is not material to an entity which makes an annual profit of CU10, 000,000.

(d) **Objectivity Convention** – This requires business entities to reflect in the financial statements, as objectively as possible, transactions as historical events. This is the main objective of historical cost accounting, although some aspects of historical cost accounting deviate from this principle, e.g. provision for depreciation which is based on the estimated useful economic life of the asset and its scrap value.

(e) **Stable Standard of Measurement** - This principle requires business entities to express all transactions in terms of a common unit of measurement namely the monetary unit (e.g. Nigeria Naira, Pounds Sterling, US Dollar, and Japanese Yen) from one accounting period to another. The financial statements prepared on historical cost basis assume that the monetary unit will remain stable. But in period of inflation, the purchasing power of the monetary unit may differ, thus affecting negatively the meaningful comparison of results obtained through historical cost accounting.

(f) **Substance over form convention** – Requires that the economic substance of a transaction be considered in reflecting it in the financial statements rather than simply based on the legal form. For instance, assets acquired on hire purchase terms or under finance leases, are recorded in the user's financial statements despite the fact that they are not owned by the user.

1.11 Accounting Concepts – These are the broad basic assumptions that underlie the periodic financial statements of a business entity. They are practical rules rather than theoretical rules and are capable of variation and evolution as accounting thought and practice develops. The Four Fundamental Accounting Concepts - which underlie the financial statements of business entity, are: Going Concern, Accrual, Consistency, and Prudence.

1.12 Accounting Convention – Is the method or procedure employed generally by accounting practitioners. Accounting convention is based on custom and is subject to changes as new developments arise. The accountant, in performing the reporting function, should follow existing accounting conventions that apply to the given situation.

1.13 Accrual Concept – At times, this is also referred to as the Matching Concept - and relates to the matching or comparing of costs with the associated revenues during a reporting period. It requires revenues to be matched with related expenses when measuring profits, revenues and expenses to be included in the Profit and Loss Account as they are earned or realised and incurred rather than when they are received and paid. Normally, revenue is recognised when realised. Revenue realisation is taken to mean the date of disposal or sale rather than the day of actual receipt of related cash. Thus, it becomes imperative to compare the revenue reported in the period with the cost or expenses incurred in earning the revenue in order to show how effectively and efficiently the resources of the entity have been used during the period. An entity is required to prepare its financial statements, other than cash flow information, on the accrual basis of accounting.

1.14 Accounting Ratio – This is usually the result of comparing two or more sets of accounting data. In most cases, this is done by dividing one of the items on the financial statement by another. Ratios help with the interpretation of financial statements by focusing on specific relationships.

1.15 Activity/Cost Drivers – Under the activity based costing (ABC), costs are assigned to outputs using activity drivers. Activity drivers are the elements that stimulate the expenditure of resources or incurrence of a cost. They help to assign operational costs to outputs based on the level of consumption or demand for activities by the individual product or service.

1.16 Accounting Entity Assumption - This is an assumption that considers the company as a legal entity separate from its owners.

1.17 Accounting Entity – Is a business or any other economic unit (including its subdivisions) that is being separately accounted for. A system of accounts is kept for the entity. An accounting entity is isolated so that recording and reporting for it are possible. Examples of accounting entities are companies, partnerships, clubs, trusts, and charities. A distinction is made between an accounting entity and a legal entity. For example, a sole proprietors accounting entity might be the business whereas the legal entity would include his personal assets. Also, in the corporate environment, affiliated or associated companies can be differently organised for legal and accounting purposes.

1.18 Accounting Software – These are programs used to maintain books of account on the computers. The software can be used to record transactions, maintain account balances, and prepare financial statements and reports. Many different accounting software packages exist, and the right package must be selected given the client's circumstances and needs. An accounting software package typically contains numerous integrated modules (for example, spreadsheet and word processing abilities). Some modules are used to account for the general ledger, accounts receivable, accounts payable, payroll, stock, and fixed assets.

1.19 Accounting System – This represents the methods, procedures, and standards followed in accumulating, classifying, recording, and reporting business activities and transactions. The accounting system includes the formal records and original source data. Regulatory requirements may exist on how a particular accounting system is to be maintained such as in the financial institutions - insurance and banking.

1.20 Cash – This is used to refer to money in hand and deposits repayable on demand with any bank (excluding overdrafts) and items that a bank will accept for immediate deposit, e.g., cheques, and money orders.

Such items as post-dated cheques, IOUs, and notes receivable are not included in the definition of cash. The cash in hand and cash on deposit in the bank are shown in the balance sheet as one figure. Cash is the most liquid of the current assets and is listed first. However, cash which are restricted in a bank account is not considered a current asset. An example is the cash held in a foreign country where remission restrictions apply.

1.21 Cash Accounting - This is the term used to describe an accounting method whereby only invoices and bills which have been paid are accounted for in the financial statements. Cash Accounting is normally used by government establishments.

1.22 Cash and Cash Equivalents – This means cash as defined and any near cash items such as marketable securities.

1.23 Cash Dividend – Is the cash payment of a share of earnings to the individual shareholders.

1.24 Cash Earnings - Refers to the excess of cash incomes over cash expenses. This is different from other earnings as it does not include non-cash expenses like depreciation or amortisation.

1.25 Cash Flow – This is an increase or decrease in the amount of cash available to a business entity. It refers to the entity's cash inflows (receipts) and outflows (disbursements) over a period of time.

1.26 Cash Flow Analysis - This is the analysis that considers the amount and timing of cash the entity received together with the timing and amount of cash it paid out. A company's cash flow position (or liquidity) can have a serious effect on the company's ability to maintain operation. This position is not necessarily shown in a cost-benefit analysis.

1.27 Cash Flow Cycle – Is a way of showing the stages or phases between paying out cash for labour, materials, etc. and receiving cash from the sale of goods or services.

1.28 Cash Flow Forecast – Is an estimate of future cash inflows and outflows of a business entity, usually prepared on a monthly basis, but covering a period of say one year to five years, depending on purpose.

1.29 Cash Flow Forecast Statement – This is a financial statement of an entity which shows the sources (inflow) and uses (outflow) of cash in a trading/accounting period. It is a prediction of all expected receipts and expenses of a business entity over a future time period which shows the expected cash balance at the end of each period. The statement is based on cash and therefore less prone to manipulation than the other main reports. It thus provides information which is not available from the balance sheets and profit and loss accounts and therefore gives a better assessment of the business performance for the accounting period – enabling users to assess the liquidity, viability, and financial adaptability of entities.

1.30 Cash at Bank - Denotes notes, coins and currency items deposited with the bank. If this is negative, i.e. a credit balance, it is called overdraft and it is a liability.

1.31 Cash Inflows – Is the sums of money received by a business entity during a period of time, say 6 months or one year.

1.32 Cash on Hand – This means notes, coins and currency items on hand. A company cannot have a negative balance of cash on hand.

1.33 Cash Outflows – This refers to the sums of money disbursed by a business during a period of time, say 6 months or one year.

1.34 Cash (Operating) Cycle – This is also known as Cash Flow Cycle. This refers to the period of time, often denoted in days, that elapses between the purchasing of the raw materials used in production, or payment for goods for resale and the receipt of payment from accounts receivable which was generated from the sale of the finished product. The shorter the period, the better for the liquidity position of the entity.

1.35 Cash Reserve Ratio (CRR) - This is the ratio of cash which individual banks need to keep on hand in the form of cash reserves with the Central Bank of the country. The CRR is calculated as a percentage of the banks demand and time deposits from customers. The purpose of CRR is to ensure both the liquidity and safety of the depositors' money with the banks. This ratio directly affects the size of the credit multiplier in the economic system.

1.36 Cash Shortage and Overage – Is a condition in which the physical amount of cash on hand differs from the book recorded amount of cash. When a business entity is involved with over-the-counter cash receipts, occasional errors may occur in making change. The cash shortage or overage is revealed when the physical cash count at the end of the day does not agree with the cash register tape. For instance, assuming that the cash count is CU800 and the cash register reading shows CU840, this shows cash shortage of CU40; this amount of cash shortage would be charged to the Cash Shortage and Overage Account. On the other hand, if the cash count at the end of the day shows CU980 and the register reading shows CU960, there is an overage of cash of CU20 which is also charged to the Cash Shortage and Overage Account. The balance in this account is either a debit or credit which is reflected in the income statement.

1.37 Financial Restructuring – This often refers to a set of processes and procedure aimed at avoiding the possible liquidation of a company. It often involves agreement with third parties or entities to help satisfy the creditors' claims under a variety of different terms and possible conditions.

1.38 Financial Reporting – Is the presentation of financial data of a company's position, operating performance, and funds flow for an accounting period. This is done by the Accountant through the process of Accounting.

1.39 International Financial Reporting Standards (IFRSs) - Focus is now on international comparability and harmonisation of standards. International Financial Reporting Standards are accounting standards set by the International Accounting Standards Board (IASB). In the European Union, IFRS is compulsory for listed companies and many national regulators have also chosen to standardise on them for all companies.

In the UK, non-listed companies have the option to either report under GAAP or IFRS, though IFRS is now mandatory for the consolidated accounts of Group companies. The US Securities and Exchange Commission require that publicly traded companies follow the US GAAP. Process is under way to harmonise the provisions of IFRS and the US GAAP. GAAP is the acronym for Generally Accepted Accounting Principles. It is the framework of guidelines that cover financial accounting, and include the standards, conventions, and rules that are followed.

1.40 Investment – This is a term with several closely-related meanings in business management, finance and economics. It relates to saving or deferring consumption. In Accounting, this is generally used to refer to the purchase of shares/stocks, real property, collectible annuities, bonds, etc, with the expectation that the company will make a capital gain, income return or both, on its disposal in the future. In Economics, Investment means expenditure on the production of goods not meant for present consumption.

1.41 Investment Appraisal/valuation – This refers to the evaluation of an investment project to determine whether or not it is likely to be viable or worthwhile.

1.42 Investment Banker – This is used to refer to an underwriter who acts as the middleman between a company that is issuing new securities and the general public.

1.43 Investment Centre – This is a responsibility centre within a business entity that has control over the revenue generated, cost and investment funds utilised. It is production or service location, function, activity or item of equipment for which costs, revenues and investments can be ascertained. It is similar to profit centre but the investment can be identified separately as well as the costs and revenues, and therefore it is evaluated through the return earned on the amount of capital invested.

1.44 Investment Goods – These are goods that are produced not for present consumption, such as capital goods, inventories, and residential housing.

1.45 Investment Manager – This refers to a person or an entity that is responsible for making the day-to-day decisions about investments.

1.46 Investment Property – An investment property is an interest in land and or buildings in respect of which construction work and development has been completed, and which is held for investment potential, any rental income being negotiated at arm's length. Investment properties are not held for consumption within the operations of the business and must not be depreciated. They are shown in the balance sheet at their open market value, and changes in value reflected in the Statement of Total Recognised Gains and Losses (STRGL)

1.47 Public financials vs. Management financials

Public financials are as reflected in annual reports and are historical data produced to regulatory requirements, presented on corporate consolidated basis with the important data often reported in notes to the statements.

Management financials are as reported to the senior management for business analysis and performance measurement, and often measured at departmental, divisional and product line level.

1.48 Reconciling Differences between Accounting Standards/Frameworks

Significance differences between accounting frameworks make it difficult to undertake comparisons of financial statements without first reconciling their differences. If comparison is required, it is necessary to first find out any major differences in accounting policies as reported in the notes to the accounts which is contained in the summary of the accounting policies used.

In accounting for the fixed assets of Property, Plant and Equipment, the US GAAP provides that Historical Cost is used and revaluations are permitted. But in IFRS, the choice can be made between Historical Cost and Re-valued Amount, and this requires regular revaluation of entire asset classes. The implication of this is that fixed assets may be held on the balance sheet at different amounts under IFRS and revaluation gains or losses may be incurred.

Similarly, in the treatment of Research & Development, the US GAAP provides that Development expenditure must be written off to the Income Statement under all circumstances; while the IFRS allows Development cost to be recognised as an asset if certain criteria are met and then amortised. This means that companies with significant development expenditure will have greater assets under IFRS.

1.49 The reason to note the different Accounting Standards

The standard principles make comparisons of the metrics between companies easier. The knowledge that two companies comply with a common standard makes it possible to perform a comparison.

Part 2

FINANCIAL REPORTING FRAMEWORKS WITH SUMMARISED GUIDANCE ON THE PREPARATION OF FINANCIAL STATEMENTS - IFRS FOR SMEs

2.1 Why IFRS for SMEs

IFRS for SMEs, through the transparency offered by a consistently applied world-wide set of financial reporting standards, has obvious advantages for the users of financial statements – the investors, lenders and those who seek to raise investment capital. Such advantages are not limited to the financial statements of companies with securities traded in the capital markets.

The IFRS for SMEs was published by the IASB (International Accounting Standards Board) in July 2009, with provision for relevant regulatory authorities in each country or territory deciding which entities are to adopt and apply IFRS for SMEs.

Three basic aims of the IFRS for SMEs are:

(1) To provide a standard for companies in countries that has no national GAAP. Here, IFRS for SMEs provides an accounting framework for companies that are not of the size nor have the resources to adopt the full IFRS.
(2) To provide the countries that already have an established national GAAP with an alternative, the IFRS standard that will be recognised and understood across different countries. This will simplify the transition to full IFRS for companies as soon as they become publicly accountable.
(3) The IASB recognised the challenge and cost to the private companies in preparing full compliant IFRS information; the users of private company financial statements may have a different focus from those interested in publicly quoted companies. IFRS for SMEs therefore attempts to meet the users' needs while balancing the costs and benefits to preparers.

IFRS for SMEs is a stand-alone standard; it does not require preparers of private company financial statements to cross-refer to full IFRS.

Compared with the full IFRS, this guide has been significantly reduced by over 85%. Much of the implementation guidance in the full IFRS has been omitted, together with the detailed explanation and requirements relating to the more complex situations not usually applicable to SMEs. The IFRS for SMEs does not only reduce the disclosure requirements, it also simplifies the recognition and measurement requirements. When there are policy options, the IFRS for SMEs generally adopts the simpler one. In itself, IFRS for SMEs is complete and contains all the mandatory requirements for SME financial statements.

The term SME (Small and Medium-sized Entity) may have different meanings and definitions in different countries. But the meaning as defined in the IFRS for SMEs is the entity that does not have public accountability and publishes general purpose financial statements. Every company has some limited accountability, at least, to its owners and the local tax authorities. Public Accountability is defined to cover any company with or that seeks to have securities traded in the stock market or that holds assets in a fiduciary capacity as its main business activity (such as banks, insurance companies, stock brokers/dealers and pension funds). Here, what is an SME is therefore based on the nature of the company instead of the size.

If a transaction is not covered by the IFRS for SMEs, the management of the company has the discretion to determine the accounting policy to apply. However, if such a transaction is covered in the full IFRS, management has the option to refer to the relevant provision of the international standard, but it is not mandatory to do so under the IFRS for SMEs.

This summary covers only the major areas of the IFRS for SMEs with explanations on the basic requirements. Any person with a reasonable level of understanding of basic accounting concepts and terms, even with little or no knowledge of the full IFRS will be able to benefit from it.

2.2 Scope
Any company which publishes general purpose financial statements for external users and does not have public accountability can adopt the IFRS for SMEs. A company has "Public Accountability" if it files or is in the process of filing its financial statements with a securities commission or other regulatory authorities for the purpose of issuing any class of financial instrument in a capital market or if, as a main part of its business activities, it holds assets in a fiduciary capacity for a wide range of third parties. Such companies as the banks, insurance companies, stock brokers and dealers and pension funds are examples of entities with public accountability as they hold assets in a fiduciary capacity. What is an SME is therefore not

based on size but on whether the entity has public accountability.

2.3 Requirement of Historical Cost - Under the IFRS for SMEs, it is a requirement that items are measured at their historical cost. It requires, however, that the revaluation of investment property and biological assets to a fair value, where the information is available. Certain categories of financial assets are also required to have their value measured at fair value. Other than those assets carried at their fair values, all items are subject to impairment or depreciation.

2.4 Concepts - IFRS for SMEs requires the financial statements to be prepared on accrual basis and on the assumption that the company will continue to exist for the foreseeable future (Going Concern - here normally assumed to be 12 months from the end of the reporting period). The major qualitative features of a useful financial statement are: understandability, relevance, materiality, reliability, substance over form, prudence, completeness, comparability, timeliness and achieving a balance between benefit and cost. The basic objective is to provide users with information about the financial performance, position and cash flows of the company useful for financial and economic decisions.

2.5 Presentation - Financial statements are required to display a true and fair view, or present fairly the financial position of the company. This requirement is achieved by adopting IFRS for SMEs and applying the major qualitative features of a useful financial statement as noted in (iv) above, i.e.: understandability, relevance, materiality, reliability, substance over form, prudence, completeness, comparability, timeliness and achieving a balance between benefit and cost. Companies are permitted to depart from the provisions of the IFRS for SMEs only on very rare circumstances, such as when management concludes that compliance would be so misleading as to conflict with the objective of the financial statements. In that case, the nature, reason and financial impact of the departure should be explained in the financial statements.

2.6 First-Time Adoption -
Fist-time adopter is the company that presents its annual financial statements in accordance with the provisions of the IFRS for SMEs for the first time. This is regardless of whether its previous accounting framework was full IFRS or another set of GAAP. There is the requirement of full retrospective application of the IFRS for SMEs effective at the reporting date for the company's first financial statement produced in line with the provisions of the IFRS for SMEs.

As an aid to transition, there are ten specific optional exemptions, one general exemption and five mandatory exceptions to the requirement of retrospective application.

The ten optional exemptions relate to: (i) Business combinations; (ii) share-based payment transactions; (iii) fair value as deemed cost for certain non-current assets; (iv) revaluation as deemed cost for certain non-current assets; (v) cumulative translation differences; (vi) provisions relating to separate financial statements; (vii) compound financial instruments; (viii) differed income tax; (ix) service concession arrangements; and (x) extractive activities.

The one general exemption from retrospective application is on grounds of impracticability. In this case, the glossary defines "impracticable" as being "when the entity cannot apply a requirement after making every reasonable effort to do so."

The five mandatory exceptions are related to the accounting that the company followed previously for: (i) de-recognition of financial assets and (ii) financial liabilities; (iii) hedge accounting estimates; (iv)Discontinued operations; (v) measuring of non-controlling interests.
Note that if a company decides not to apply the IFRS for SMEs in some future period and then later reverts to it, the concessions on first-time adoption are no longer available.

2.7 Selection of Accounting Policies - Where the IFRS for SMEs does not specifically provide for a transaction, event or condition, a company has the discretion to develop and apply an accounting policy. This information must be relevant to the users' needs and must be reliable. "Reliability" means that the financial statements represent faithfully the financial position, financial performance and cash flows of the company, reflect the economic substance of transactions, and are neutral, prudent and complete in all material aspects.

2.8 Financial Statements

2.8.1 What they are
These are the reports containing financial information about a business entity. Based on the reporting standards, a complete set of financial statements comprises: (i) a Statement of Financial Position (Balance Sheet); (ii) either a single Statement of Comprehensive Income and Expenses or a separate Income Statement (Profit and Loss Account); (iii) a Statement of

Changes in Equity (SOCIE); (iv) a Statement of cash flows; and (v) Explanatory Notes to the financial statements (including the accounting policies and supplementary schedules).

There is no prescribed format to be adopted. However, the Implementation Guidance for the IFRS for SMEs includes a full illustrative set of financial statements and disclosure checklist. There are minimum disclosures to be made on the face of the financial statements as well as in the notes. Financial statements disclose corresponding information for the preceding period (known as "Comparatives"), unless there is a compelling reason not to.

2.8.2 Objective of Financial Statements –
The objective of financial statements is to provide information about the financial position, performance and changes in the financial position of an entity. This information is useful to a wide range of users in making economic decisions – i.e. financial and investment decisions.

2.8.3 Financial Decisions – refer to business decisions that may involve:
- Determining the proper amount of funds to be used in the company;
- Selecting projects and the analysis of capital expenditure;
- Raising funds on the most favourable terms possible; and
- Managing working capital such as goods stock and accounts receivable.

2.8.4 Users of Financial Statements and Accounting Information: - These include External and Internal users, namely:
- The Stakeholders group made up of existing and potential shareholders.
- The Loan Creditors made up of present and potential debenture holders, loan stock and providers of short-term loans and finance.
- The Employees consisting of the existing, potential and past.
- The Financier Advisers, financial analysts, economists, statistician, researchers, trade unions, and stockbrokers.
- The Business Contacts such as customers, suppliers, competitors and business rivals, and credit rating agencies.
- The Government and its agencies, especially the tax and local authorities.
- The Public including the taxpayers, ratepayers, consumers, pressure groups, etc.

2.8.5 Uses of Accounting Information:
- For Planning – to evaluate the financial effects of possible alternative courses of future action.

- For Decision-making – e.g. in resource allocation and relocation and whether to undertake a project or not.
- For Performance Assessment and Control – to monitor the performance, products, personnel and department of an entity.

2.8.6 Responsibility for Financial Statements - The management of a business entity has the primary responsibility for the preparation and presentation of financial statements.

2.8.7 Qualitative Characteristics of Financial Statements - These are the attributes that make the information in financial statements useful to the users – investors, creditors, analysts, and others:

- Relevance
- Reliability
- Comparability
- Understandability

2.9 Financial Statement Analysis - Is a method used by interested parties such as investors, creditors, and management to evaluate the past, current, and projected conditions and performance of the company. Ratio analysis is the most common form of financial statement analysis. It provides relative measures of the company's financial conditions and operating performance.

2.10 Statement of Financial Position (Balance Sheet) - This is the financial statement which presents a company's assets, liabilities and equity at a selected point in time usually the date to which the income statement is made up; it is a "snapshot" showing the assets and liabilities at that particular point in time. The balance sheet is divided into two equal parts – a part showing the Capital and Liabilities, and the other showing the Assets. It thus reflects any of the following expressions of the accounting equation:
- Assets = Capital + Liabilities; or
- Assets = Liabilities + Shareholders' Equity; or
- Assets = Capital employed = Liabilities, or
- Assets – Liabilities = Ownership interest; or
- Assets - liabilities = Contributions from owners + Gains – Losses – Distributions to owners; or
- Current Assets + Non-current Assets = Equity + Non-current liabilities + Current liabilities.

(a) The financial position of a company is affected by the economic resources it controls, its financial structure, its liquidity and solvency, and its capacity to adapt to changes in the environment in which it operates. The balance sheet provides this kind of information.

(b) An asset is a resource controlled by an entity as a result of past events and from which future economic benefits are expected to flow to the entity.

(c) A liability is a present obligation of the entity arising from past events, the settlement of which is expected to result in an outflow from the entity of resources embodying economic benefits.

(d) Equity is the residual interest in the assets of the entity after deducting all its liabilities.

Assets and liabilities are classified as Current and Non-Current, and they are presented as separate classifications in the statement of financial position, unless presentation based on liquidity provides reliable and more relevant information.

An asset is classified as current if it has the following characteristics: (i) is expected to be realised, sold or consumed in the entity's normal operating cycle (irrespective of length); (ii) it is primarily held for the purpose of trade; (iii) it is expected to be realised within twelve months after the end of the reporting period; (iv) it is cash or cash equivalents.

A liability is classified as current if it meets the following criteria: (i) it is expected to be settled during the entity's normal operating cycle; (ii) it is primarily held for the purpose of being traded; (iii) it is due to be settled with twelve months after the end of the reporting period; or (iv) the entity does not have an unconditional right to defer settlement of the liability until at least twelve months after the end of the reporting period.

As a minimum, the following items are presented in the statement of financial position.

Assets: (i) Property, Plant and Equipment - PPE; (ii) Investment Property; (iii) Intangible assets; (iv) Financial assets; (v) Investments; (vi) Biological assets – living animals and/ or plants; (vii) Deferred tax assets; (viii) Current tax assets; (ix) Inventories (Goods Stocks); (x) Trade and other receivables; and (xi) Cash and Cash Equivalents.

Equity: (i) Equity attributable to the owners of the Parent Company; (ii) Non-controlling Interests (Minority Interests) presented separately from the owners' equity interests.

Liabilities: (i) Deferred tax liabilities; (ii) Current tax liabilities (iii) Financial liabilities; (iv) Provisions; and (v) Trade and other Payables.

2.11 Statement of Comprehensive Income and Expenses (SOCIE) and Income Statement

2.11.1 Income Statement - This is the entity's Profit and Loss Account and shows its financial performance. It is the statement showing the elements used in arriving at the net income for the accounting period (i.e. Revenues less Expenses equal Profit/Loss).

2.11.2 Statement of Comprehensive Income and Expenses (SOCIE)/ Statement of Recognised Income and Expenses (SORIE): - A company can decide to present its total comprehensive income and expenses in one or two financial statements: A single statement of comprehensive income showing all items of income and expenses of the period in the one statement; or The two-statement method consisting of an income statement (detailing all items of income and expenses recognised in the period except those recognised outside the profit and loss), and a statement of comprehensive income (which presents the items recognised outside profit and loss.)

Changing between one and two statements is a change in accounting policy and should be reported as such.

By function, SORIE is an extended form of the Income Statement and like the Statement of Cash Flows it shows changes in the company's financial position. It is a primary statement required (in the UK) for a "true and fair view", which brings together all recognised gains and losses for the period. It covers the profit or loss for the period as shown in the profit and loss account together with all other movements in reserves - recognised gains and losses - attributable to the shareholders (thus reflecting changes in the net assets and equity between periods). It thus has a wider content than the profit and loss account.

2.11.3 Elements of the Statement of Comprehensive Income and Expenses - Irrespective of the approach followed - a single statement of comprehensive income or the two-statement approach - the following items, as a minimum, are detailed in the income statement:

Revenue; Finance costs; Share of profit or loss of associates and Joint-Ventures accounted for under the equity method; Tax expense; A single item consisting of the total of (a) the post-tax profit or loss of discontinued operations, and (b) the post-tax gains or loss recognised on the measurement of fair value less costs of sale or on the disposal of the net assets comprising the discontinued operation, and profit and loss for the period.

The statement of comprehensive income starts with the profit or loss for the period and includes each item of other comprehensive income, the share of the other comprehensive income of associates and jointly controlled companies and total comprehensive income.
Under the single statement approach, the same details are included in the single statement, which must include a sub-total of profit or loss for the trading period.

In both approaches, profit or loss for the period is apportioned to the amount attributable to non-controlling interest and to the owners of the parent company.

If there are other items relevant to the understanding of the company's financial performance, then additional lines or subheading are added.
An analysis of total expenses is shown using a classification based on either the nature or function of expenses within the company, whichever provide reliable and more relevant information.

2.12 Material, Extra-ordinary and Exceptional items - IFRS for SMEs requires the separate disclosure of items of income and expenses that are material. Materiality refers to the importance of an item or other information which inclusion in the statement or otherwise has an influence on decision making and the value or price of the company's shares.

An item is **extra-ordinary** if it is both unusual in nature and infrequent in occurrence. It is a material item, profit or loss, which arises as a result of an event outside the normal trading activities of the business entity. It is abnormal in its amount and is not expected to recur. Such an item is not associated with normal operations, and since 2004 it is no longer permitted under the IFRS for SMEs, though under the US-GAAP, such items can still be shown in the profit and loss account under Unusual and Infrequent items.

Exceptional items are different from extra-ordinary items. These are material non-recurring but not unusual items of income and expense arising from circumstances such as: write-downs of inventories to net realizable value or of property, plant and equipment to recoverable amount, as well as reversals of such write-downs; restructurings of the activities of an entity; disposals of property, plant and equipment; disposals of associates or other financial assets; discontinued operations; onerous contracts; and litigation settlements. Disclosure may be in the statement of comprehensive income or in the notes.

2.13 Statement of Changes in Equity - This presents a reconciliation of equity items between the start an end of the reporting period.
Items included in the statement of changes in equity are as follows:

1. Total comprehensive income for the period, showing separately the total amount attributable to the owners of the parent company and to non-controlling interests (i.e. minority interests)
2. For each component of equity: the effects of changes in accounting policies and corrections of material prior-year errors.
3. For each component of equity: a reconciliation between the carrying amount at the start and end of the period, separately disclosing changes resulting in (a) profit or loss (b) each item of other comprehensive income, (c) transactions with the owners that do not result in a loss of control.

The details of distributions, the balance of retained earnings and a reconciliation of the carrying amount of each class of equity and each item recognised directly in the equity are presented either in the statement of changes in equity or in the notes to the financial statements.

2.14 Statement of income and retained earnings - To many companies, the only changes to the equity during the period under review will be in: the income/profit for the year, retained earnings at the beginning of the year, dividends declared and paid or payable during the year, reinstatement of retained earnings for the purpose of correcting the prior-year errors, reinstatement of retained earnings as a result of changes in the accounting policy applied, and retained earnings at the end of the year. If this is the case, the company is permitted to present a statement of income and retained earnings instead of both the statement of comprehensive income and statement of changes in equity. However, if the company is using the two performance statement approach, the requirement for an income statement still stands.

2.15 Statement of cash flows - This shows the sources and uses of cash – as relate to the operating, investing, and financing activities - during the reporting period. The statement measures the cash flows, reflecting changes in cash available – changes in the financial position of the company; it is based on cash and therefore less prone to manipulation. It thus provides information which is not available from the balance sheet and profit and loss account and therefore gives a better assessment of the business performance for the reporting period – enabling users to assess the liquidity, viability, and financial adaptability of the reporting company.

The operating activities are associated with the company's principal revenue-generating operations. The investing activities are related to the acquisition and disposal of long-term assets, including business combinations and investments. The financing activities are those on changes in equity and borrowings.

A company may decide to produce the cash flows statement by using either of the two approaches: The Direct Method, or The Indirect Method.
• **The Direct Method** shows the actual operating gross cash receipts and gross payments that make up the net cash flow from operating activities. The main advantage of this method is that it shows only the operating cash receipts and payments.
• **The Indirect Method** starts with operating profit and adjusts for non-cash items to reconcile it to the net cash flow from operating activities (i.e. adjusting the net profit or loss for non-operating and non-cash transactions, and for changes in working capital).The major advantage of this method is that it highlights the differences between the operating profit and net cash flow from operating activities.
Cash flows from investing and financing activities are reported separately gross.

Non-cash activities include impairment losses or reversals, depreciation, amortisation, unrealised fair value gains and losses, and provision charges in the income statement.

2.16 Notes and supplementary schedules to the Financial Statements -
These contain further details on the numbers that appear on the face of the financial statements and should always be referred to in any financial analysis and interpretation. They can provide both clarification of what figures in the statements refer to and also additional explanation and quality of the figures.

- They explain items in the balance sheet and income statement;
- They disclose the risks and uncertainties affecting the entity; and
- They explain any resources and obligations not recognised in the balance sheet.

As a minimum, IFRS for SMEs requires that the following be disclosed within the notes to the financial statements:
- A statement of compliance with the IFRS for SMEs
- Accounting Policies adopted.
- Critical Accounting estimates and adjustments
- Information not presented in the primary statements but required by the IFRS for SMEs, and

Where applicable, changes in accounting policies, changes in accounting estimates and information about externally imposed capital requirements are also disclosed.

2.17 Accounting policies, estimates and errors - Where IFRS for SMEs specifically addresses a transaction, event, or condition, the company applies that provision of IFRS for SMEs. If, however, it does not, the company is to use its judgement to determine and apply an accounting policy that results in information that satisfies the qualitative characteristics of financial statements as earlier explained (under Concepts). Where there is no appropriate guidance, the company considers the applicability of the sources as follows in descending order: the requirements and guidance in the IFRS for SMEs for similar and related issues; and the definitions, recognition criteria and measurement concepts for assets, liabilities, income and expenses in the section under Assets and Liabilities. The company may also, but not mandatory, consider the full IFRS. All accounting policies chosen and applied are to be applied consistently and over similar transactions and events.

The changes in accounting policies as a result of an amendment to IFRS for SMEs standard are accounted for in accordance with the transition provisions of the amendment. If specific transaction provisions do not exist, the company is to follow the same procedures as for correction of prior-period errors (as shown below.) Where the IFRS for SMEs provides a choice of accounting policy for a specific transaction and the company changes its choice, this is a change of accounting policy and is to be reported as such.

2.18 Critical Accounting Estimates and Judgements - A company is to disclose the nature and carrying value of those assets and liabilities for which judgements, estimates and assumptions have a significant risk of causing a material adjustment to the carrying values within the next financial period.

Changes in the accounting estimates are recognised prospectively by including the effects in profit or loss in the period affected – that is, the period of the change and the future periods where relevant, except if the change in the estimate gives rise to changes in assets, liabilities or equity. In this case, it is recognised by adjusting the carrying value of the related asset, liability or equity in the period of the change.

2.19 Correction of prior-period Errors - Errors may arise from mistakes and oversights or misinterpretation of available information. Material prior-period errors are adjusted retrospectively i.e. by adjusting opening retained earnings and related comparatives. The exception to this requirement is when it is impracticable to determine either the period-specific effect or the cumulative effect of the error. In this latter case, the company corrects such errors prospectively from the earliest date practicable. The error and effect of its correction on the financial statements are disclosed.

2.20 Related Parties - The main categories of related parties are:
Subsidiaries, Fellow subsidiaries, Associates, Joint Ventures, Key Management personnel of the company and its parent (including their close family members), Parties with control or Joint Control or Significant influence over the entity (including close family members where applicable), and Post-employment benefit plans.

Related parties exclude finance providers and governments in the course of their normal dealings with the company. Another exemption from the disclosure requirement is where there is a state control over the company.
The names of the immediate parent and the ultimate controlling parties, an individual or group of individuals, are reported irrespective of whether there have been transactions with those related parties.

Where there have been related party transactions, disclosure is made of the nature of the relationship, the value of transactions, and outstanding balances and other elements necessary for a clear understanding of the financial statements, e.g. volume and amount of transactions, amount outstanding and pricing policies. The disclosure is made by certain categories of related party and by major types of transaction. Items of a similar nature may be disclosed in aggregate, for instance, short-term employee benefits, except when separate disclosure is necessary for an understanding of the effects of related party transactions on the company's financial statements.

Disclosures that related party transactions were made on terms equivalent to those that prevail in arm's length transactions are made only if such terms can be substantiated.

2.21 Events after the End of the Reporting Period - Events after the end of the reporting period may qualify as adjusting events or non-adjusting events.

(a) **Adjusting events** provide further evidence of conditions that existed at the end of the reporting period and lead to adjustments to the financial statements. Examples of adjusting events are: the news that a debtor has become insolvent and a valuation of a company's freehold offices which indicates a permanent reduction in value below the balance sheet amount. Adjusting events give rise to changes in the accounts figures and should be reflected in the financial statements.

(b) **Non-adjusting events** relate to conditions that arose after the end of the reporting period and do not lead to adjustments, only to disclosures in the financial statements. Examples include: subsequent merger, labour disputes, and a new share issue. Non-adjusting events are disclosed by way of notes to the accounts.

Dividends proposed or declared after the end of the reporting period are not recognised as a liability in the reporting period. Management discloses the date on which the financial statements were authorised for issue and who gave that authorisation. If the owners or persons have the power to amend the financial statements after issue, this fact is also disclosed.

2.22 Balance Sheet Elements: Assets and Liabilities

2.22.1 By the accounting equation, the assets of the company (financial and non-financial assets) equal its liabilities (what the company owes, including to its shareholders).

Expressed differently:

Current assets + Non-current assets
=
Equity + Non-current liabilities + Current Liabilities

Current Assets:

Cash and Cash Equivalents
Other Current Assets
Trade Receivables
Inventories

Non-current Assets:

Available-for-sale investments
Investments in Associates
Other Intangibles
Goodwill
Property, Plant and Equipment

EQUAL TO

Equity:

Share Capital
Other Reserves
Retained Earnings
Minority Interest

Plus

Liabilities – Non-Current

Long-term Borrowings
Deferred Tax
Long-term Provisions

Plus

Liabilities – Current:

Trade and other Payables
Short-term Borrowings
Current portion of Long-term Borrowings
Current tax payable
Short-term Provisions

2.22.2 Assets and Liabilities

1. An asset is a resource controlled by an entity as a result of past events and from which future economic benefits are expected to flow to the entity.

2. A liability is a present obligation of the entity arising from past events, the settlement of which is expected to result in an outflow from the entity of resources embodying economic benefits.

3. Non-Financial assets:

(i) Inventories -
Inventories are originally recognised at cost. The cost of inventories includes all costs of purchase, costs of conversion and other costs incurred in bringing the inventories to their present location and condition.

Cost of purchase includes the purchase price, import duties, non-refundable taxes, transport and handling costs and any other directly attributable costs less trade discounts, rebates and similar items.

Subsequently, inventories are valued at the lower of (i) cost and (ii) selling price, less costs necessary to complete and sell.

The cost of inventories used is assigned by using either the first-in, first-out (FIFO) or weighted average cost method of costing. Last-in, first-out (LIFO) is not permitted. The same costing method is used for all inventories that have a similar nature and use to the company. Different cost methods may be justified where inventories have a different nature and use.

(ii) Investment Property -
Investment property is a property – land or a building, or part of a building or both – held by the owner or by the lessee under a finance lease to earn rentals or for capital appreciation or both. A property interest held for use in the production or supply of goods or services or for administrative purposes is not an investment property, nor is an interest held for sale in the ordinary course of business.

The cost of a purchased investment property is its purchase price plus any directly attributable costs, such as professional fees for legal services, property transfer taxes and other transaction costs.

Subsequently, investment property is measured at fair value, with changes in fair value recognised in profit or loss, where the fair value can be measured reliably without undue cost or effort.

Where fair value is no longer available without undue cost or effort, the property is deemed to be an item of property, plant and equipment and its accounting follows accordingly. The company should use the latest available fair value as its deemed cost until a reliable measure of fair value becomes available again.

When an investment property interest is held under a lease, only the interest in the lease is recognised, not the underlying property.

Where an investment property is carried at cost, the property is treated as part of PPE. Transfers to or from investment property apply when the property meets or ceases to meet the definition of an investment property

(iii) Property, Plant and Equipment (PPE) -
PPE is made up of tangible assets that (a) are held for use in the production or supply of goods and services, for rental to others or for administrative purposes; and (b) are expected to be used during more than one period. This also applies to investment property carried at cost as a result of undue cost or effort preventing it being carried at fair value.

PPE is initially measured at cost, which includes: (a) the purchase price, including legal and brokerage fees, import duties and other non-refundable taxes (net of discounts and rebates); (b) any directly attributable costs to bring the asset to the present location and condition necessary for it to be capable of operating in the manner intended by the company; and (c) the initial estimate of the costs of dismantling and removing the item and restoring the site on which it is located.

Subsequently, classes of PPE are carried at cost less accumulated depreciation and any accumulated impairment losses. The depreciable amount of an item of PPE, being the gross carrying value less the estimated residual value, is depreciated on a systematic basis over its economic useful life.

PPE may have significant parts with different useful lives. Depreciation is calculated based on each individual part's life. Major parts that have the same useful life and depreciation method may be grouped in determining the depreciation charge.

The cost of a major inspection or replacement of parts of an item occurring at regular intervals over the useful economic life is capitalised to the extent that it meets the recognition criteria of an asset. The carrying amount of the previous inspection or parts replaced is derecognised.

(iv) Intangible Assets (other than Goodwill) -
An intangible asset is an identifiable non-monetary asset without physical substance. The identifiability criterion is satisfied when the intangible asset is separable, i.e. it can be sold, transferred, licensed, rented or exchanged, or where it arises from contractual or other legal rights. Expenditure on intangibles is recognised as an asset when it satisfies the recognition criteria of an asset.

Intangible assets are measured initially at cost. Cost includes (a) the purchase price – including import duties and non-refundable purchase taxes, net of trade discounts and rebates; and (b) any costs directly attributable to preparing the assets for its intended use.

Internal expenditure incurred on intangible assets, including any expenditure for research and development activities, is recognised as an expense, unless that expense forms part of the cost of another asset that meets the asset recognition criteria in the IFRS for SMEs. In such a case, the expenditure is added to the asset and measured subsequently in accordance with the requirements of the IFRS for SMEs.

The recognition criteria are strict. Most costs relating to internally generated intangible items cannot be capitalised and are recognised as an expense as incurred. Examples of such costs include start-up costs, training, advertisement and relocation costs, Expenditure on internally generated brands, mastheads, customer lists, publishing titles and items similar in substance are not recognised as assets.

Intangible assets are carried at cost less any accumulated amortisation and any accumulated impairment losses. Intangible assets are amortised on a systematic basis over the useful lives of the intangibles. The useful life is determined based on the contractual period of the asset or on other legal rights and cannot be indefinite, Where the company cannot determine the useful life, that life is presumed to be 10 years. The residual value of such assets at the end of their useful lives is assumed to be zero, unless there is either a commitment by a third party to purchase the asset or there is an active market for the asset.

(v) Financial Instruments -
A financial instrument is any contract that gives rise to both a financial asset of one company and a financial liability or equity instrument of another company. A financial instrument is recognised when the company becomes a party to its contractual provisions.

The IFRS for SMEs classifies the financial instruments requirements into two sections: Section 11 on basic financial instruments; and section 12 on additional financial instrument issues. Section 11 applies to all companies within the scope of the IFRS for SMEs; section 12 only affects larger and more complex companies.

The management of a company has a choice of either applying the provisions of sections 11 and 12 of the IFRS for SMEs or applying the recognition and measurement provisions of IAS 39 – "Financial Instruments: Recognition and Measurement," but the disclosure requirements of the IFRS for SMEs.

Most likely, the accounting policy choice of opting for IAS 39 will only be taking by companies that belong to groups where the parent reports under full IFRS.

(vi) Basic Financial Instruments -
The basic financial instruments are: Cash; simple debt instruments – such as loans payable or receivable; a commitment to receive a loan; and an investment in non-convertible preference shares and non-puttable ordinary and preference shares.

A debt instrument qualifies as basic financial instrument if it meets the following conditions:
1. Unleveraged returns to holders that are easily determinable;
2. No contractual provision that could, by its terms, result in the holder losing the principal amount or interest attributable to the current or prior periods;
3. Contractual terms that permit early repayment are not contingent on future events; and
4. No conditional returns or repayment provisions other than those listed above.

Examples of basic debt instruments include demand deposits, accounts and loans payable and receivable, commercial paper, bonds and similar debt instruments.

When first recognised, a basic financial instrument is measured at transaction price, unless the arrangement is in effect a financing transaction. In this case, it is the present value of the future payment discounted using a market rate. Subsequently, at the end of each reporting period, basic financial instruments are measured as follows:

- Debt instruments at amortised cost using the effective interest rate method.
- Commitments to receive a loan at cost – which could be nil – less impairment.
- Investments in non-convertible or non-puttable shares at fair value if the shares are publicly traded or fair value can be measured reliably, otherwise at cost less impairment.

2.23 Fair value -
Fair value is calculated in accordance with the following hierarchy:

- The quoted price for an identical asset in an active market.
- If no active market exists, the price of a recent transaction for an identical asset.
- If neither of the above two applies, by use of a valuation technique.

2.24 Impairment of financial instruments measured at cost or amortised at cost -
Where there is any objective evidence of impairment of financial assets measured at cost or amortised cost, an impairment loss is recognised immediately in profit or loss. For an instrument measured at amortised cost, the impairment loss is the difference between the asset's carrying amount and the present value of estimated cash flows discounted at the asset's original effective interest rate. Where an asset is measured at cost less impairment, the impairment loss is the difference between the asset's carrying amount and the best estimate of the amount that the company would receive for the asset in a sale at the reporting date.

2.25 De-recognition of financial assets -
A company can only derecognise a financial asset when:
- The rights to the cash flows from the assets have expired or are settled;
- The company has transferred substantially all the risks and rewards relating to the financial asset; or
- It has retained some significant risks and rewards but has transferred control of the asset to another party. The assets are therefore derecognised, and any rights and obligation created or retained are recognised.

2.26 De-recognition of financial liabilities -
Financial liabilities are derecognised only when they are extinguished – i.e. when the obligation is discharged, cancelled, or expires.

2.27 Further Issues relating to financial instruments -
All financial instruments within the scope of section 12 are measured at fair value both on initial recognition and at each reporting date except for situations where there is no longer a reliable measure of fair value. In this case, a company continues to carry that instrument at its last available fair value, which is treated at cost, subject to impairment, until the instrument is derecognised or its fair value becomes available.

2.28 Hedge accounting -
A company may establish a hedging relationship, designating a hedging instrument and a hedged item in such a way that the following criteria are met and apply hedge accounting. This means that the gain or loss related to the hedged risks on the hedged item and hedging instrument are recognised in profit or loss at the same time.
A hedging instrument:

• Can take the form of an interest rate swap, a foreign currency swap, a foreign currency or commodity forward exchange contract that is expected to be highly effective in offsetting the risk designated as the hedge risk.
• Involves a party external to the entity.
• Has a notional amount equal to the designated amount of the principal or notional amount of the hedged item.
• Has a specified maturity date no later than the maturity of the item being hedged, the expected settlement of a commodity transaction being hedged or the occurrence of the highly probable forecast transaction being hedged.
• Has no pre-payment, early termination, or extension facilities.

To qualify for hedge accounting, a company:

• Documents at the inception of the hedge relationship between designated hedging instruments and hedged items;
• Identifies the risk hedged as: (i) an interest rate risk; (ii) a foreign exchange rate in a firm commitment or a highly probable forecast transaction, or in a net investment in a foreign operation; or (iii) a price risk of commodity; and
• Expects the hedging instrument to be highly effective in offsetting the designated hedged risk.

The effectiveness of a hedge is the degree to which changes in fair value or cash flows of the hedged item that are attributable to the hedged risk are offset by changes in the fair value or cash flows of the hedging instrument.

For a fair value hedge (hedge of fixed interest risk or of commodity price risk of a commodity held), the hedged item is adjusted for the gain or loss attributable to the hedged risk. That element is included in profit or loss to offset the impact of the hedging instrument.

Gains and losses on instruments qualifying as cash flow hedges (hedges of variable interest rate risk or foreign exchange risk, or hedge of a net investment in a foreign operation) are included in equity and recycled to profit or loss when the hedged item affects profit or loss, or are used to adjust the carrying amount of an asset or liability at acquisition.

2.29 Impairment of non-financial assets -
Assets are subject to an impairment test according to the requirements of following outline, except: deferred tax asset, employee benefit assets, financial assets, investment properties carried at fair value, and biological assets carried at fair value less estimated cost to sell.

1. **Impairment of inventories**: These are assessed for impairment at each reporting date by comparing the carrying value with the selling price less cost to complete and sell. Company then reassesses the selling price, less cost to complete and sell in each subsequent period to determine if the impairment loss previously recognised should be reversed.
2. **Impairment of assets other than inventories**: Here asset is impaired when the recoverable amount is less than the carrying value. The reduction is an impairment loss and is recognised immediately in the profit and loss account.

For assets, including goodwill, they are assessed for impairment where there is an indication that the asset may be impaired. Existence of impairment indicators is assessed at each reporting date. The external indicators of impairment include a decline in asset's market value, significant adverse changes in the technological, market, economic or legal environment, increases in the market interest rates, or when the company's net asset value is above the value that might be expected in a sale of the company. The internal indicators include evidence of obsolescence or physical damage of the asset, changes in the way an asset is used, such as restructuring of discontinued operations, or evidence from internal reporting that the economic performance of an asset is, or will be, worse than expected.

In performing the impairment assessment of an asset, company estimates the fair value less cost to sell. The best evidence for this is a price in a binding sale agreement in an arm's length transaction or a market price in an active market. In the absence of that, the value is based on the best available information to reflect the amount that a company could obtain at the reporting date from disposal of the asset in an arm's length transaction between knowledgeable, willing parties, less costs of disposal.

For goodwill, the fair value is derived from measurement of the fair value of the larger group assets to which the goodwill belonged. For this purpose of impairment assessment, goodwill acquired in a business combination is allocated from the acquisition date to each of the acquirer's cash-generating units that is expected to benefit from the synergies of the combination, irrespective of whether other assets or liabilities are assigned to those units.

During each reporting date after recognition of the impairment loss, company assesses whether there is any indication that an impairment loss may have decreased or may no longer exist. The impairment loss, other than goodwill, is reversed if their fair value less cost to sell exceeds its carrying value. The amount of the reversal is subject to certain limitations. Goodwill impairment canner be reversed.

2.30 Provisions and Contingencies -
1. **Recognition and initial measurement** – A provision is recognised only when: the company has a present obligation to transfer economic benefits as a result of a past event; it is probable (more likely than not) that the company will be required to transfer economic benefits in settlement of the obligation; and the amount of the obligation can be reliably estimated.

The amount recognised as a provision is the best estimate of the amount required to settle the obligation at the reporting date. Where material, the amount of the provision is the present value of the amount expected to be required to settle the obligation.

A present obligation arising from a past event may take the form of a legal or constructive obligation. An obligating event leaves the company no realistic alternative to settling the obligation. If the company can avoid the future expenditure by its future actions, then it has no present obligation, and no provision is required.

If some or the entire amount required to settle a provision is reimbursed by another party, the company recognises the reimbursement as a separate asset only when it is virtually certain that it will receive the reimbursement on settlement of the obligation. The reimbursement receivable is presented on the settlement of financial position as an asset and is not offset against the provision. The amount of expected reimbursement is disclosed in the financial statements. Net presentation is allowed in the statement of comprehensive income.

Company reviews provisions at each reporting date and adjusts them to reflect the current best estimate of the amount that would be needed to settle the obligation at that reporting date.

2. **Contingent Liabilities**: A contingent liability is either a possible but uncertain obligation or a present obligation that is not recognised as a liability because either it is not probable an outflow will occur or the amount cannot be measured reliably. A company does not recognise, but discloses, a contingent liability as a liability unless it has been acquired in a business combination.

3. **Contingent Assets**: Contingent assets are not recognised in the financial statements. When the realisation of benefits is virtually certain, the related asset is not a contingent asset but meets the definition of asset and it is recognised as such.

2.31 Employee Benefits - What is included?

Employee benefits include all forms of consideration given by the company in exchange for the services rendered by the employees. These benefits include salary-related benefits (such as wages, salaries, profit sharing, bonuses, long-service leave and share-based payments), termination benefits (such as severance or redundancy pay), and post-employment benefits (such as retirement benefit plans).

The post-employment benefits include pensions, termination indemnities, post-employment life insurance, and post-employment medical care. Pensions and termination indemnities are provided to the employees through their defined contribution plans or defined benefit plans. Whether an arrangement is a defined contribution or a defined benefit plan depends on the terms and conditions.

A defined contribution plan is a pension plan under which the company pays fixed contributions into a fund held by a separate entity.

The company has no legal or constructive obligation to pay further contributions if the plan does not hold sufficient assets to pay all employees benefits relating to employee service in the current or prior periods. A defined benefit plan is a pension plan that is not a defined contribution plan.

For multi-employer and State plans which are classified as defined contribution or defined benefit plans depending on the terms, special consideration needs to be given. Where there is insufficient information available to use defined benefit accounting, defined contribution accounting is applied with additional disclosures made.

The cost of defined contribution plans is the contribution payable by the employer for the accounting period.

For the defined benefit plans, the accrued benefit valuation method (i.e. the projected unit credit method) is required to be used for calculating the defined benefit obligations when a company is able to do so without undue cost and effort. In this method, each period of service is considered to give a rise to an additional unit of benefit entitlement, and each unit is measured separately to build up the final obligation

Where the project unit method is not used because of undue cost and effort, the company is allowed to measure its obligations by making some simplifications by ignoring estimated future salary increases, future services and possible in-service mortality of current employees.

It is a normal practice for companies to engage the services of an actuary to perform the actuarial valuation needed to calculate its defined benefit obligation. However, the IFRS for SMEs does not require an actuary to be engaged. The defined benefit obligation is recorded at present values, taking into account the future salary increases and using a discount rate derived from the yield on high-quality corporate bonds with a maturity consistent with the expected maturity of the obligations. Where this is not possible, the yield on government bonds is used.

Assets held by long-term employee benefit fund and qualifying insurance policies are referred to as plan assets. These plan assets are subtracted from the defined benefit obligation to determine the net defined benefit liability. If this results in net asset (surplus), this surplus can only be recognised to the extent that a company is able to recover the surplus either through reduced contributions in the future or through refunds from the plan.

The costs relating to defined benefit plans are recognised in the profit or loss, unless the company chooses to recognise actuarial gains or losses in Other Comprehensive Income (OCI), i.e. the part of the cost that relates to the re-measurement of the liability can be presented in the Other Comprehensive Income statement, but all other elements of the cost are recognised in the income statement.

The IFRS for SMEs also covers other long term benefits, including long-service and sabbatical leave, jubilee and other long-service benefits, long-term disability benefits and compensation and bonus payments made after 12 months or more after the end of the period in which they are earned. They are recognised as liabilities and are measured at the present value of the benefit obligation at the reporting date, less the fair value of any plan assets out of which obligations are to be settled directly.

2.32 Income Taxes -
The current tax is recognised as a current liability for tax payable on taxable profit for the current and past periods. It is measured at an amount that includes the effect of possible review by the tax authorities. The following are recognised;

(i) A deferred tax liability for temporary differences that are expected to increase taxable profit in the future;
(ii) A deferred tax asset for temporary differences that are expected to reduce taxable profit in the future; and
(iii) A deferred tax asset for the carry-forward of unused tax losses and unused tax credits. This applies to all such items except for: (a) unremitted earnings of investments in foreign subsidiaries, branches, associates, and joint ventures, provided that the investment is of a permanent duration and it is unlikely that the temporary difference will reverse in the foreseeable future; and (b) a temporary difference arising from initial recognition of goodwill.

Temporary deferred tax differences arise in a number of situations, for instance, among others:
(i) Where differences occur between the tax base of an asset or a liability and its carrying amount in the accounts.
(ii) Where an item is recognised in the computation of profit for tax purposes in one accounting period and is recognised in the statement of comprehensive income of another period.

Current and deferred tax is recognised as a tax expense in profit or loss, unless the tax arises from an item recognised as other comprehensive income or directly in equity. In this case, the tax follows the recognition basis of the item from which it arises.

Deferred tax assets and liabilities are measured at the tax rates that are expected to apply to the period when the asset is realised or the liability is settled, based on the tax rates and tax laws that apply or have been enacted or subsequently enacted by the end of the reporting period. Deferred tax assets and liabilities are not discounted. Company recognises a valuation allowance against deferred tax assets that are not likely to be recovered.

Where a company is subject to different tax rates depending on different levels of taxable income, deferred tax assets and liabilities are measured at the average enacted or subsequently enacted tax rate applicable to the periods in which it expects the deferred tax asset to be realised or deferred tax liability to be settled.

Tax relating to dividends that is paid or payable to taxation authorities on behalf of the owners (e.g. Withholding tax) is charged to equity as part of the dividends.

2.33 Leases
A lease is an agreement in which the lessor conveys to the lessee in return for a payment or a series of payments the rights to use an asset for an agreed period of time. At the inception, a lease is classified as a finance lease if it transfers to the lessee substantially all of the risks and rewards incidental to ownership. All other leases are treated as operating leases. Whether a lease is a finance lease or an operating lease depends on the substance of the transaction rather than the legal form of the contract.

For sale-and-lease-back transactions resulting in a lease-back of a finance lease, any gain realised by the seller-lessee on the transaction is deferred and amortised through the profit or loss over the lease term. Where the transaction results in an operating lease and the transaction is at fair value, any profit or loss is recognised immediately or deferred and amortised over the period the asset is expected to be used.

In the Books of the Lessee -
A lessee in a finance lease records an asset and a liability in the financial statements at amounts equal to fair value of the leased property, or, if lower, at the present value of the leased property. The lessee depreciates this asset in accordance with its depreciation policy for similar assets or

over the lease term if shorter. The lessee apportions minimum lease payments between finance charge and reduction of the outstanding liability.

The lessee in an operating lease records the rental payments as expense on a straight-line basis over the lease term unless either another systematic basis is more representative of the time pattern of the user's benefit or the payments are structured to increase with expected general inflation.

In the Books of the Lessor
The lessor records an asset leased under a finance lease at an amount equal to the net investment in the lease. This is the gross investment in the lease, discounted at the interest rate implicit in the lease. The lessor records operating lease assets according to the nature of the assets and depreciates them on the basis consistent with the normal depreciation policy for similar owned assets. Rental income is recognised on a straight-line basis over the lease term unless either another systematic basis is more representative of the time pattern over which the benefit of the leased asset is diminished or the payments are structured to increase with the expected general inflation.

2.34 Business combinations, consolidated financial statements, and investments in associates and joint ventures

2.34.1   Business Combinations -
Business combinations are the bringing together of separate companies or businesses into one entity. Here, an acquirer is identified in all cases, and the entity obtains control of one or more other companies or businesses called acquire. Control means the power to govern the financial and operating policies of a company in order to benefit from its activities.

The structure of a business combination can take a variety of forms to take advantage of legal, taxation or other reasons. It may entail the purchase of the equity of another company; the purchase of all the net assets of another company; the assumption of the liabilities of another company; or the purchase of some of the net assets of another company that combined forms one or more businesses. This may be achieved by the issue of equity instruments, the transfer of cash, cash equivalents, or other assets, or a combination of any. The transaction may be between the shareholders of the combining companies or between one company and the shareholders of another company. It may also entail the establishment of a new company to control the combining companies or net assets transferred, or the restructuring of one or more of the combining companies.

Business combinations between companies under common control are not covered by the IFRS for SMEs. All business combinations are accounted for by applying the purchase method. The steps in applying the purchase method are:

(i) Identify the acquirer;
(ii) Measure the cost of the business combination; and
(iii) Allocate the cost of the business combination to the assets acquired and liabilities and contingent liabilities assumed at the acquisition date.

The cost of business combination includes the fair value at the date of exchange of assets given, liabilities incurred or assumed and equity instruments issued by the acquirer, in exchange for control of the acquire, and directly attributable costs. These costs are allocated at the acquisition date by recognising the acquiree's identifiable assets, liabilities and contingent liabilities at their fair value at that date, except for non-current assets that are classified as held for sale. These are measured at fair value less cost to sell

In recognising the items acquired, the following criteria are followed:

(a) Assets other than intangible assets are recognised when it is probable that any associated future economic benefits will follow to the acquirer and their fair value can reliably be measured.
(b) Liabilities other than contingent liabilities are recognised when it is probable that an out flow of resources will be acquired to settle the obligation and their fair value can be reliably measured.
(c) Intangible assets or contingent liabilities are recognised when their fair value can reliably be measured.
The goodwill (i.e. the excess of the cost of the business combination over the acquirer's interest in the net fair value of the identifiable assets, liabilities and contingent liabilities) is recognised as an intangible asset at the acquisition date. After the initial recognition, the goodwill is measured at cost less accumulated amortisation and less any accumulated impairment losses. The useful life of goodwill cannot be indefinite; where a company is unable to make a reliable estimate, the life is presumed to be 10 years.
Negative goodwill is recognised in profit or loss immediately after the company has assessed the identification and measurement of identifiable items arising on acquisition and cost of the business combination.

2.34.2 Consolidated and Separate Financial Statements -

A subsidiary is a company that is controlled by the parent (holding company). Control is assumed to exist when the parent holds more than 50% of the company's voting power. This assumption may be rebutted if there is clear evidence to the contrary. All subsidiaries are consolidated. A subsidiary is consolidated from the date of acquisition until the date on which the parent ceases control of the subsidiary. The consolidated financial statements present the financial information about the group as a single economic unit. This process requires the application of the consolidation procedures, elimination of the intra-group balances and transactions, and the application of uniform reporting date and accounting policies.

The parent presents consolidated financial statements unless it is itself a subsidiary. The ultimate or intermediate parent of the company produces consolidated financial statements either in accordance with full IFRS or in line with the IFRS for SMEs, or it has no subsidiaries other than any acquired with the intention of sale or other disposal within one year.

A special purpose entity (SPE) is a company created to accomplish a narrow, well-defined objective. A company consolidates an SPE when the substance of the relationship between the company and the SPE shows that the SPE is controlled by the company.

Separate financial statements are those financial statements presented by a parent, or an investor in which the investments are accounted for as direct equity interests, rather than by inclusion of reported results and net assets of the investees. When a parent prepares separate financial statements, the investments in subsidiaries, jointly controlled companies and associates are accounted for either at cost or at fair value through profit or loss.

Combined financial statements are a single set of financial statements of two or more companies with common objectives and economic interest, and controlled by a single investor. If a company prepares combined financial statements as conforming to the IFRS for SMEs, those statements must comply with all of the requirements of the standard, including elimination of inter-company transactions and balances, and application of same reporting date and accounting policies.

2.34.3 Investments in Associates -

An associate is a company over which the investor has significant influence but which is neither a subsidiary nor a joint venture of the investor. Significant influence means the power to participate in the financial and operating policy decisions of the associate but is not control or joint control over those policies. It is assumed to exist when the investor holds at least 20% of the investee's voting power. It is also assumed not to exist when less than 20% is held. These assumptions may be rebutted if there is clear evidence to the contrary.

Associates are accounted for consistently using the cost model (i.e. cost less any accumulated impairment losses), the equity method or the fair value through profit or loss model. Investments in associates are classified as non-current assets.

2.34.4 Investments in Joint Ventures -
A joint venture refers to a contractual agreement whereby two or more parties (called the venturers) undertake an economic activity that is subject to joint control. Joint control is defined as the contractually agreed sharing control of an economic activity. A venture accounts for its investment based on the type of joint venture arrangement such as: jointly controlled assets or jointly controlled companies.

For jointly controlled operations, this entails operations that involve use of the assets and other resources of the venturers rather than the establishment of a separate company. Each venturer uses its own property, plant and equipment, carries its own inventory, and incurs its own expenses and liabilities. The joint venture agreement usually provides a means by which the revenue from the sale of the joint venture product and any expenses incurred in common are shared among the venturers. Each venture recognises in the financial statements the assets that it controls and the liabilities that it incurs, as well as the expenses that it incurs and its share of the income that it earns from the sale of goods or services by the joint venture.

In a holding or jointly controlled assets joint venture, the ventures have joint control of assets contributed or acquired for the purpose of the joint venture. A venturer recognises in its financial statements its share of the jointly controlled assets, any liabilities that it has incurred, its share of any liabilities incurred jointly with the other venturers in relation to the joint venture, together with its share of any expenses incurred by the joint venture and any expenses that it has incurred in respect of its interest in the joint venture.

For a jointly controlled company arrangement, the joint venture involves the establishment of a separate company in which each venture has an interest. The contractual arrangement between the venturers establishes joint control over the economic activity of the company. The venture reports in its financial statements its interest in a jointly controlled company as follows:
(1) At cost, less any accumulated impairment losses;
(2) Using the equity method; or
(3) At fair value through profit or loss.

The gains or losses on contribution or sale of assets to a joint venture by a venturer reflect the substance of the transaction. They are recognised to the extent of the interests of the other venturers, provided the assets are retained by the joint venture and significant risks and rewards of ownership of the contributed assets have been transferred. The venture recognises the full amount of any loss when there is evidence of impairment loss from the contribution or sale.

2.35 Liabilities and Equity-
What is Equity? Equity means the residual interest in the company's assets after deducting all its liabilities. Equity includes investments by the owners of the company, plus additions to those investments earned through profitable operations and retained over the years for use in the company's activities, minus reductions to the owners' investments as a result of unprofitable operations and distributions to the owners.

What is a Liability? A liability represents a current obligation of a company arising from past events that is expected to result in the outflow of economic benefits from the company.

Some instruments issued by a reporting company may have the legal form of shares but in real terms are debts. They are reported as liabilities except in certain strictly defined conditions for puttable instruments (Puttable instruments are those financial instruments that give the holders the right to put them back to the issuer for another financial assets (such as cash). Put procedure could be automatic in case of retirement or death of a holder, or in case of any uncertain future events.)

2.35.1 Issue of Equity Shares -
Equity instruments such as ordinary shares are measured at fair value of cash or other resources received, net of transaction costs and related income tax benefit.

1.35.2 Compound Financial Instruments -
On issuing convertible debt or similar compound instrument that contain both a liability and an equity component, a company allocates the proceeds between the liability component and the equity component at initial recognition.

2.35.3 Treasury Shares -
Treasury shares are equity instruments that have acquired or re-acquired by the company. A company deducts from equity the fair value of the consideration given for the treasury shares. The company does not recognise a gain or loss in profit or loss on the purchase, sale, or issue or cancellation of treasury shares.

2.35.4 Non-controlling interest
In consolidated financial statements, any non-controlling interest in the net assets of the subsidiary is included in the equity.

2.36 Income and Expenses

2.36.1 Revenue:
Revenue is measured at the fair value of the consideration received or receivable. Revenue is recognised when it is probable that the economic benefits will flow to the company and these benefits can be reliably measured.

Revenue from rendering service is recognised when the outcome of the transaction can be estimated reliably by reference to the stage of completion of the transaction. Revenue is recognised in the accounting periods in which the services are rendered under the percentage-of-completion method.

A transaction is not a sale and revenue is not recognised when, for example, the company retains an obligation for unsatisfactory performance not covered by normal warranty provisions, the receipt of revenue from a particular sale is contingent on the buyer selling the goods, or the buyer has the power to rescind the purchase for a reason specified in the sales contract and the company is uncertain about the probability of return.

Where a company operates a loyalty award scheme, it allocates the fair value of the consideration received or receivable in respect of the initial sale between the award credits and the other components of the sale.

It may be necessary to apply the recognition criteria to the separately identifiable components of a single transaction to reflect the substance of the transaction. An instance is when a product's selling price includes an identifiable amount for subsequent servicing in which case a portion is deferred and recognised as revenue over the period during which the service is performed.

The interest income is recognised using the effective interest rate method. Royalties are recognised on the accrual basis in accordance with the substance of the relevant agreement. Dividends are recognised when the shareholders' right to receive payment is established.

If the result of the construction contract can be estimated reliably, the revenue and contract costs associated with the contract are recognised as revenue and expenses respectively by reference to the stage of completion of the contract operations at the end of the reporting period. Where the result of the contract cannot be estimated reliably, recognition of the revenue can only be made to the extent of contract costs incurred that is probable will be recovered. The contract costs should be recognised as an expense in the period in which they are incurred.

2.36.2 Government Grants -

A government grant is assistance by government in the form of a transfer of resources to a company in return for past or future compliance with specified conditions relating to the operating activities of the company.

Government grants exclude assistance that cannot reasonably have a value placed on it and transactions with government that cannot be distinguished from normal trading transactions of the company. The company recognises government grants according to the nature of the grants as follows:

(i) A grant that does not impose specified future performance conditions on the recipient is recognised in income when the grant proceeds are receivable.
(ii) A grant that imposes specified future performance conditions on the recipient is recognised in income only when the performance conditions are met.
(iii) Grants received before the income recognition criteria are satisfied are recognised as a liability.
Company measures grants at the fair value of asset received or receivable.

2.36.3 Borrowing Costs -

Company recognises all borrowing costs as expenses in profit or loss in the period in which they are incurred.

2.36.4 Share-based Payment -

Share-based payments cover transactions that may be settled by some form of equity instrument (e.g. Shares), or cash or other assets where the amount payable is based on the price of the company's shares or by some combination of the two.

Company recognises the goods or services received in a share-based payment transaction when it gets the goods or as the services are received. Share-based payments granted to employees are recognised over the period of service that must be completed before they have become unconditionally entitled to the award.

Equity-settled share-based payment transactions are measured by reference to the fair value of the goods and services received, unless the fair value cannot be reliably estimated, or they are transactions with employees. In that case, their value is measured, and the corresponding increase in equity, by reference to the fair value of the equity instruments granted.

Where getting fair value is impracticable, the company use its judgment to apply the most appropriate valuation method to obtain fair value. Cash-settled share-based payments are measured at the fair value of the liability.

Equity-settled share-based payments are not re-measured except to incorporate the effect of non-market vesting conditions. The liability arising from cash-settled share-based payments is re-measured at the end of each reporting period and at the date of settlement, with changes in fair value recognised in profit or loss.

2.37 Currencies

2.37.1 Functional Currency (CU) -

All components of the financial statements are measured in the currency of the primary economic environment in which the company operates i.e. its functional currency. All transactions entered into in currencies other than the functional currency are treated as transactions in a foreign currency.

2.37.2 Foreign currency transactions -

A transaction in a foreign currency is recorded in the functional currency using the exchange rate at the date of the transaction – average rates may be used if they do not fluctuate significantly. At the end of the operating period, foreign currency monetary balances are reported using the exchange rate at the end of the reporting period. Non-monetary balances denominated in a foreign currency and carried at cost are reported using the exchange rate at the date of the transaction. Non-monetary items denominated in a foreign currency and carried at fair value are reported using the exchange rate at the date when the fair values were determined.

Exchange differences are recognised as profit or loss for the period, except for those differences arising on a monetary item that forms part of a company's net investment in a foreign company – subject to strict criteria of what qualifies as net investment. In the consolidated financial statements, such exchange differences are classified separately in equity. They are not recognised in profit or loss upon disposal of the net investment.

2.37.3 Presentation Currency -

Company may choose to present its financial statements in any currency. If the presentation currency differs from the functional currency, the company translates its results and financial position into the presentation currency. If the functional currency is not the currency of a hyperinflationary economy, the assets and liabilities are translated at the closing rate at the end of the reporting period; the statement of comprehensive income is translated using the exchange rates at the dates of the transactions. All resulting exchange differences are recognised as a separate component of equity.

When preparing consolidated financial statements that involve more than one company, the companies in the group may have different functional currencies. The financial statements of all the companies are translated into the company's presentation currency. The exchange differences arising from the translation in respect of each company are recognised in other comprehensive income.

2.38 Hyperinflation

Hyperinflation is indicated by characteristics of the economic environment of a country. One of the indicators that an economy is hyperinflationary is if the cumulative inflation rate over three years is approaching or exceeds 100%

Where a company's functional currency is the currency of a hyperinflationary economy, the financial statements are stated in terms of the presentation currency at the end of the reporting period. The corresponding figures for the previous period are also stated in terms of the measuring unit current at the end of the reporting period. The gain or loss on the net monetary position is included in profit or loss and disclosed separately.

2.39 Specialised Activities

2.39.1 Agriculture -
A company that is involved in agricultural activities measures its biological assets at fair value less estimated point-of-sale costs, where such fair value is readily available or determinable without undue cost or effort. Where fair value is not used, the company measures such assets at cost less any accumulated depreciation and any accumulated impairment losses. The agricultural produce harvested from the biological assets is measured at fair value less estimated costs to sell at the point of harvest.

2.39.2 Extractive Industries -
A company using IFRS for SMEs that is involved in an extractive industry recognises exploration expenditure as an expense in the period in which it is incurred. Companies accounting for expenditure on the acquisition or development of tangible and intangible fixed assets for use in the extractive activities follow the guidance in the IFRS for SMEs, section 17 (Property, Plant and Equipment) and section 18 (Intangible Assets other than Goodwill). When a company has obligation to dismantle or remove an item or restore a site, it follows the guidance in the IFRS for SMEs section 17 and 21 (Provisions and Contingencies).

2.39.3 Service Concession Arrangements -
A service concession is an arrangement in which the government or other public sector body (called the grantor) contracts with a private operator to operate and maintain the grantor's infrastructure, such as roads, bridges, tunnels, airports, energy distribution networks, prisons and hospitals. Concession arrangements fall into two broad categories, which determine the accounting method that applies:
(i) The operator recognises a financial asset to the extent that it has an unconditional contractual right to receive cash or another financial asset from or at the direction of the grantor. The financial asset is measured at fair value. The company then follows the accounting for other financial instruments (section 11 and 12 of the IFRS for SMEs).

(ii) The operator recognises an intangible asset to the extent that it receives a right (a licence) to charge users of the public service. The intangible asset is measured at fair value. The company then follows the accounting for intangible assets (section 18 of IFRS for SMEs).

2.40 A Standard Format for Balance Sheet presentation under IFRS (IAS1)

This is a standard format:

ABC GROUP – BALANCE SHEET AS AT 31 DECEMBER 20X10

	CU
Current Assets :	
Inventories (Stocks)	3,000
Trade Receivables (Trade Debtors)	400
Other Current Assets	200
Cash & Cash Equivalents	400
Total Current Assets	4,000
Non-current Assets:	
Property, Plant and Equipment (PPE)	9,000
Goodwill	2,000
Other Intangible Assets	400
Investments in Associates	600
Available-for-sale investments	200
Total non-current assets	12,200
Total Assets	16,200
Equity and Liabilities:	
Equity attributable to equity holders of the parent-	
Share Capital	4,000
Other Reserves	2,200
Retained Earnings	400
Minority Interest	600
Total Equity	7,200

Non-current Liabilities:	
Long-term Borrowings	2,000
Deferred Tax	1,800
Long-term Provisions	200
Total Non-current Liabilities	4,000
Current Liabilities:	
Trade and other payables (Trade Creditors)	1,000
Short-term Borrowings	2,000
Current portion of Long-term Borrowings	1,200
Current Tax Payable	200
Short-term Provisions	600
Total Current Liabilities	5,000
Total Equity and Liabilities	16,200

2.41 Balance Sheet Elements - what they indicate about the company and their link to strategy and decision.

2.41.1 Current Assets
• Inventory (Stock) – The quantity held will be determined by a combination of factors – the company's purchasing and logistics capability and its manufacturing and sales lead times. It can be indicative of the company's supply chain strategy (e.g. just-in-time or reduced holding cost) and manufacturing and sales processes (e.g. lean sales).
• Trade Receivables (Debtors) – level will be driven by the company's attitude to credit risk (credit policy) and its ability to enforce collection, which in turn may be impacted by value chain position and the bargaining power of the customers.
• The general aim of any company is to turn stock into debtors as quickly as possible and turn debtors into cash as quickly as possible.
• Effective management of current assets is critical to liquidity; and in most industries, current assets should at least equal current liabilities.

2.41.2 Non-current Assets
• Tangible Fixed Assets: A high volume of tangible fixed assets (PPE) values on the balance sheet can be an indication of asset-intensive industry and potentially high barrier to entry for competitors.

- Significant expenditure on PPE also limits the flexibility of a company to manage change and heightens its potential vulnerability to say political instability in a country where it has significant investments.
- The fixed assets included in the balance sheet may not reflect the true assets of the company, e.g. assets may increase in value but may be shown at historical cost less depreciation. Some companies may not show most of their assets on their balance sheet.
- Even if there is no revaluation of property, plant and equipment undertaken (which is allowed under IFRS), net PP & E values represented on the balance sheet have been adjusted for depreciation (refer to the notes).

2.41.3 Equity
- Share Capital – This indicates the extent to which the company has relied on selling shares to raise capital (as opposed to borrowing from lenders). Selling shares transfers ownership and control of the company but reduces the company's exposure to debt and interest obligations.
- Retained Earnings – represents the accumulation of all historic profits generated by the company, less monies used for reinvestment in the business and dividends paid to shareholders.
- Minority Interest - represents the level of shares not held by the holding company of a subsidiary; it is the book value of the outside shareholders' interest in the subsidiary company. The existence of minority interest means that the subsidiary is not wholly owned by the holding/parent company.

2.41.4 Non-current Liabilities
- Long term borrowings - If a company depends on long term debt (usually debt owed fore greater than one year) it is an indication of its financial strategy and access to capital sources. The ratio of debt to equity, known as gearing, indicates a company's strategy for raising finance.
- Debt is typically more expensive than equity. This is because, lenders are guaranteed a return (interest) on their investment; but the dividends paid on equity are typically discretionary.
- Debt is more tax efficient than equity, as the interest paid are tax deductible while dividends paid on equity are made after tax had been deducted.
- Debt does not impact on ownership and control of the company.
- However, debts do place an increased pressure on a business as the company has no choice but to pay agreed interest, and eventually repay the debts.

2.41.5 Current Liabilities
- Trade Payables – The level of trade payables indicates the value chain position and the consequent bargaining power of the suppliers, as well as the trade credits negotiated.
- Short-term borrowings (such as overdrafts) – are impacted by both management strategies on capital structure and the market factors such as interest rates. Short-term borrowings are typically required to help manage the working capital.

2.42 Income Statements
Income statements show the performance of the company during the accounting period under review. Profit for the period represents the surplus between revenue and expenses. This is available for reinvestment in the business (as retained earnings) or payment to the shareholders (as dividends).

- Performance - is the ability of a company to earn a profit on the resources that have been invested in it. Information about the amounts and variability of profits helps in forecasting future cash flows from the company's existing resources and in forecasting potential additional cash flows from additional resources that might be invested in the company.
- The accounting framework states that information about performance is primarily provided in an income statement.
- Incomes - are the increases in the economic benefits during the accounting period in the form of inflows or enhancements of assets or decreases of liabilities that result in increases in equity, other than those relating to contributions from equity participants.
- Expenses – are decreases in economic benefits during the accounting period in the form of outflows or depletions of assets or establishment of liabilities that result in decreases in equity, other than those relating to distributions to equity participants.

An income statement can be presented in a number of ways; a company may decide to look at expenses grouped by functions or may also choose to classify expenses by nature. The standard structure by function of expenses grouping is as follows.

2.43 Example of an Income Statement (expenses grouped by function)

ABC Limited
Income Statement for the year ending 31 December 20X10

Revenue	CU 6,000.00
Cost of sales	3,200.00
Gross Profit	2,800.00
Other income	600.00
Distribution costs	(200.00)
Administrative expenses	(200.00)
Other expenses	(100.00)
EBITDA	2,900.00
Depreciation & Amortisation	(200.00)
EBIT	2,700.00
Finance costs (interests)	(300.00)
Share of profit of associates	100.00
Profit before Tax (PBT)	2,500.00
Income tax expense	(400.00)
Profit for the year (PAT)	2,100.00

Notes:

- EBITDA (Earnings before interest, taxes, depreciation and amortisation) is approximate to net cash from operations – therefore, it is a useful measure to compare operating performance across companies.
- EBITDA reflects how well the business is managed based on current operations, without the impact of financing decisions – i.e. it's operating performance.
- Retained Earnings – the investors in the company choose, either by voting or by empowering the management, how much of the profit to reinvest into the business and how much to distribute to shareholders.
- Dividends are distributions to shareholders as payment for the use of their capital (i.e. return on their investment).
- Surplus earnings are retained in the business to be reinvested in future periods.

The first part of the Income Statement looks at sales and costs associated with the company's trading activities. What are the drivers of these metrics?

2.44 Drivers of Cost and Revenue
• Revenue- This is driven by the price and volume of the goods and services sold, which in turn is influenced by the pricing strategy (premium and discount extended) and market share or market volume. Ordinarily, a lower price attracts higher sales volume and a larger market share will generate a greater volume of sales.
• Cost of sales – This is made up of manufacturing costs - materials, direct labour, and direct expenses (i.e. plant burden) – or for a services company, all direct service costs – mainly direct labour.
• Labour costs – Are driven by wages and size of the workforce.
• Manufacturing costs – comprise the costs of materials plus the costs associated with manufacturing, i.e. the use of property, plant and equipment.
• From the Gross Profit, other income is added and other indirect expenses taken away. The drivers of these metrics are as follows:
• The structure of the business (e.g. need for high Research and Development, global physical presence).
• Type of business – for instance, large operational footprint (manufacturing), largely people cost (consulting), significant product development, marketing, sales and distribution costs (consumer business, retail).
• Company attitude towards costs (for instance, a company focussing on its overheads as the era of high gross profit is getting over).
• The competitiveness of the market in which the company operates (for instance, supermarkets need to be lean as margins on low value products are tight and competition keep price down).

2.45 **In analysing the key financial statements** (Income Statement and Balance Sheet) -
• It is important to understand what the definitions are; how to interpret them; and what pitfalls to watch out for.
• A financial and or investment decision maker, before taking decision, is expected to always interpret financial statements to obtain an understanding of the company's finances; look at trends in the company's finances over time; and compare one company's finances to another's.
• Besides looking at the key elements in the financial statements, the effective decision maker will also need to calculate and interpret key financial ratios.

Part 3

FINANCIAL/ACCOUNTING RATIOS, ANALYSIS AND INTERPRETATION

3.1 Horizontal Analysis: The simplest way to analyse the financial statements is by what is known as Horizontal Analysis. This involves the comparing of the current year's results with that of the previous year, noting and rationalizing any major changes. A line by line approach, that is, to be meaningful, it must be carried out while recognising the change in turnover and the relevance of any other information known about the company.

In reality, the analyst will find such other information in:
(a) The directors' report,
(b) The chairman's report, or
(c) The newspaper cuttings about the company and/or the industry in which it does business.

For the student in the examination hall, these other information are usually obtained from the opening sentences of the question where what the company does and why the question of interpreting the accounts are stated. The notes following the numerical information also provide such further details. To give a satisfactory answer to the question, the student must ensure that such other additional information are utilised – referring to and using the points to analyse the observed trends.

In interpreting the results detailed in the Profit and Loss Account, for instance, a change in turnover supports the analysis. In a 40% increase in turnover, we could anticipate a 40% increase as well in other variables in the profit and loss account. Balance sheet changes, such as inventories and debtors, can be rationalised in similar manner. Assuming the gross profit failed to increase with the turnover, we need to establish the reason why – could it be as a result of increase in the purchase costs (cost of sales), or the writing down/off of the inventories, or other cost allocation to the cost of sales such as research and development cost?

3.2 As an illustration, say BDD Ltd in 2010 reported net profit and sales figure of CU100,000 and CU800,000. In 2011, net profit increased to CU180,000 and sales for the year amounted to CU1,800,000. The net profit percentage earned by TJ Ltd, a company that carries on trade in completion with BDD Ltd, was 14% in 2011.

Required: Calculate and comment on the net profit percentages of BDD Ltd for 2010 and 2011.

Here, the company's accounts report a significant increase in net profit, but the accounting ratios show that the net profit expressed as a percentage of sales has declined; moreover, it is well below the return earned by a comparable business.

Net profit percentages	**2010**	**2011**
100,000/800,000 x 100%	12.5%	
180,000/1,800,000 x 100%		10%

We cannot make a definitive assessment of BDD's progress on the basis of a single accounting ratio, but it does point to the need for further investigation to determine why the ratio has fallen and why the margin earned by its competitor has not been achieved.

At the point of the Operating Profit, many more factors may need to be considered. Should the breakdown of the expenses be provided, a further line by line comparison becomes inevitable. Remember that some costs are fixed or semi-fixed and therefore not expected to increase with turnover (e.g. depreciation cost) whilst other costs are variable (e.g. distribution cost and commission.) In arriving at the operating profit, many significant items which may affect the analysis may have included, such as:
- Depreciation of tangible fixed assets
- Amortisation of intangible assets including goodwill
- Government grants received
- Exceptional items
- Research and development costs
- Advertising expenditure
- Directors' emoluments
- Staff costs which may have increased over the time in line with inflation
- Etc.

From operating profit is derived the profit before tax after including two additional items of Investment Income and Interest Payable. These items may not likely increase with turnover. However, a simple periodic comparison may expose other changes such as increase in borrowing, leasing charges, and changes in investment portfolios.

These figures may align with the balance sheet and there is the need to check them against the level of borrowings (bank overdraft inclusive) and the investments portfolios held (both current and fixed.)

For the Profit after Tax which follows the profit before tax, it is useful to determine the rate of tax by comparing the tax charge to the profits. Ordinarily, the rate should be fairly constant from year to year. Consideration should also be had on the policy of the company with regard to deferred tax provisioning.

The current dividend payments should be compared to those of the previous periods. A fall in dividend payments for a publicly quoted company gives a disturbing signal about its operations even when the profit for the year has also declined. Accordingly, major companies usually try to avoid this if at all possible.

Using the metrics detailed in the financial statements, key ratios are calculated to provide an indication of a company's absolute and relative performance in many areas. This technique is the next level after the horizontal analysis and the most common form of financial statement analysis. It is called "Ratio Analysis".

3.3 Financial/Accounting Ratio Analysis – Is a technique used by interested parties such as investors, creditors, and management to evaluate the past, current, and projected conditions and performance of a company. It provides relative measures of the company's conditions and performance.

Generally, in answering examination questions, ratio analysis should only be used where the question specifically asked for the use of ratios. And in that case, if no particular ratios are mentioned, you have to make a choice of the ratio to use.
When using the financial ratios, the analyst makes two types of comparisons:
(a) Industry comparison – using the industry average. Here, the ratios of a company are compared with those of similar companies in the industry or with industry averages or norms to determine how the company is faring relative to its competitors.
(b) Trend analysis. In this case, the company's present ratio is compared with its past and stated or expected future ratios to determine whether the company's financial condition is improving or deteriorating over time.

3.4 Illustrative Example: PKZ Limited

(Note: this example is used as a basis of calculating the ratios as indicated in this Part)

Towards the end of 2010, the directors of the company, PKZ Ltd, a company of wholesale merchants, decided to raise additional capital in the form of a debenture of CU1,600,000 to facilitate expansion of their business.

The annual financial statements for the year ended 2011, together with the corresponding figures for 2010 are as set below:

Trading and Profit and Loss Account

		2010		2011
		CU'000		CU'000
Credit sales		11,000		13,200
Cash sales		1,000		800
		12,000		14,000
Less: Opening stock	2,680		2,720	
Credit purchase	9,400		11,340	
Closing stock	(2,720)		(3,000)	
Cost of sales		9,360		11,060
Gross Margin		2,640		2,940
Expenses: Administration	540		550	
Selling	790		800	
Distribution	560		650	
Depreciation	60		70	
		1,950		2,070
Operating profit		690		870
Less: Debenture Interest		-		160
Net Profit		690		710
Corporation tax		345		355
Net profit after tax		345		355

Movement of Reserves
Reserves at 1 January	1,310	1,500
Add: Net Profit after tax	345	355
	1,655	1,855
Less: Dividends proposed	155	155
Reserves at 31 December	1,500	1,700

Balance Sheet as at 31 December

		2010	2011
		CU'000	CU'000
Fixed assets:			
Cost		1,400	1,800
Accumulated depreciation		300	370
		1,100	1,430
Current assets:			
Stock	2,720		3,000
Trade debtors	1,920		3,120
Cash at Bank	40		240
	4,680		6,360
Less: Current Liabilities			
Trade creditors	780		980
Taxation	345		355
Dividends payable	155		155
	1,280		1,490
Working capital		3,400	4,870
		4,500	6,300
Less: Debentures		-	1,600
		4,500	4,700

Share Capital	3,000	3,000
Reserves	1,500	1,700
	---------	---------
	4,500	4,700
	=====	=====

The following additional information is provided:

1. At 1 January 2010, trade debtors amounted to CU1,600,000, gross assets to CU5,420,000 and shareholders' equity to CU4,310,000.
2. The product range and buying prices were unchanged over the period 1 January 2010 to 31 December 2011.
3. The debenture loan was received on 1 January 2011 and additional warehouse facilities became available on that date at a cost of CU400,000.
4. No fixed assets were purchased during the year 2010.

3.5 An Accounting Ratio involves measuring the numerical relationship between two balances appearing in the financial statements. There are varieties of ratios that could be calculated. So it is best to define your need and restrict the calculations by being selective.

3.6 Principal Accounting Ratios

In general, the principal analytical ratios are: ROCE (Return on Capital Employed), Profit Margin, Current or Quick ratio, and Gearing Ratio. And the three broad classifications of traditional accounting ratios are:

Class A: Profitability & Asset Efficiency

What is reflected: The performance of company and its managers, including the efficiency of asset usage in profit generation – is the business more or less profitable than its peers/or its previous performance?

Examples:
(a) ROCE – shows how efficiently a company uses its resources, how well the company generates profit for its creditors or shareholders and thus a key ratio in assessing financial achievement.
(b) Gross Profit %/ Operating margin/Net profit margin – Shows how profitable the business is compared to its peers or its past.
(c) Stock/inventory Turnover and
(d) Debtors and Creditors days – show how well the company manages its working capital.

(e) Asset turnover/Fixed Asset turnover – shows how efficiently the company is using its assets to generate revenue.

Class B: Financial Stability & Leverage

What is reflected: Financial structure and stability of the Company.

Examples:
(a) Gearing Ratio and
(b) Interest Cover – show how reliant the company is on loans compared to equity.
(c) Current Ratio and
(d) Liquidity/ Quick Ratio – show whether the company has enough current assets to pay off its short term liabilities.
(e) Proprietary ratio - Indicates the degree to which unsecured creditors are protected against loss in the event of liquidation.

Class C: Investment (Investors)

What is reflected: Relationship of the number of ordinary shares and their price to the profits, dividends and assets of the Company.

Examples:
(a) EPS
(b) P/E Ratio
(c) Dividend Yield
(d) Dividend Cover
(e) Net Assets per Share

The big advantage of ratios is that they provide the metrics for comparing a business's performance year on year, or with its competitors. In this case, what really is important is the relationship between the numbers rather than the numbers themselves. However, it is important to remember that, although, a useful tool, ratio analysis does have some limitations – it does not always take into consideration the impact of inflation, nor does it account for the effect of the use of different accounting policies adopted by the companies.

The management of the company are likely to be concerned about all the aspect of its business and may therefore want to know all the major ratios in each category.

For shareholders or potential investors, the primary concern may be with the investment ratios, though some financial stability and profitability measures are likely to be of interest to them. And for creditors, they may be more interested in the financial stability of the company, a financial like the bank acting as the primary source of finance may also be concerned with its profitability.

In interpreting ratios, note that, on their own, they have limited use. Most of the marks in an examination questions will be for sensible, well explained and accurate comments on the major ratios. One should be able to comment sensibly by finding answers to questions such as these:
• What does the ratio mean?
• The change in the ratio, what does it mean?
• What is the normal expectation?
• What are the major limitations of the ratio?

As an outside analyst may not have access to all the facts available to management, in practice, they will be limited in the analysis they can perform by the level of information available. Similarly, in any examination question, the level of information provided will be limited.

3.7 Financial Profitability & Assets Turnover Ratios - calculations

3.7.1 ROCE (Return on Capital Employed) – This is also known as the Primary Ratio as it is often the most important measure of profitability. ROCE is a key business objective and reflects the earning power of the business, showing how efficiently a company uses its resources, how well the company generates profit for its creditors or shareholders and thus a key ratio in assessing financial achievement. If the return is low, it may be better for the company to realise some of its assets and invest the proceeds in high interest yielding ventures as a low return can easily become a loss if the company suffers a decline.

$$ROCE = \frac{Profit}{Capital\ Employed} \times 100\%$$

The two main factors affecting ROCE are Profitability of sales and the Rate of Asset Utilisation. The product of these two gives the return on capital employed:

(i)

$$\frac{\text{Operating profit}}{\text{Sales}} \times \frac{\text{Sales}}{\text{Operating Assets}} = \frac{\text{Operating Profit}}{\text{Operating Assets}} = \text{ROCE}$$

(ii)

Operating Profit Margin x Asset Turnover = ROCE

Alternative calculations of Return on Capital Employed are:

(a) Return on Shareholders' Equity (this is more relevant to existing and potential shareholders).

Return on Equity =
$$\frac{\text{Profit after interest and other preference dividends}}{\text{Ordinary Share Capital + Reserves}} \times 100\%$$

(b) Overall Return (used by managers to assess performance) =
$$\frac{\text{Operating Profit}}{\text{Share Capital + Reserves + all borrowings}} \times 100\%$$

For **PKZ Ltd**, the formula can be used to shed more light on its performance.

Profit Margin x Asset Utilisation = Return on gross assets

2010: ROCE (i) = $\{\frac{690}{12{,}000} \times 100\%\} \times \frac{12{,}000}{[1/2(5{,}420 + 5{,}780)]}$: 1

= 5.75% x 2.14 = 12.31%

2011: ROCE (i) = $\{\frac{870}{14{,}000} \times 100\%\} \times \frac{14{,}000}{[1/2(7{,}380^* + 7{,}790)]}$: 1

= 6.21% x 1.85 = 11.50%

Note*: Assets at the end of 2010 totalled CU5,780,000, but cash of CU1,600,000 was received from a debenture issue made on 1 January 2011. This is included in the opening balance for the purpose of computing average total assets during the year 2011.

From the calculation, it is apparent that a major reduction in asset utilisation has occurred, and this could be as a result of the longer credit period allowed to customers in the year 2011.

3.7.2 Gross Profit Percentage – the margin that a company makes on its sales and it is given as:

$$\frac{\text{Gross Profit}}{\text{Turnover}} \times 100\%$$

This is expected to remain fairly constant, though changes may be attributable to changes in the selling prices, sales mix, purchase cost in carriage and discounts, production cost in material, labour and overheads, and stocks – errors in counting, valuation, cut off, and stock shortages.

Low margins generally suggest poor performance but may be as a result of expansion costs or the company trying to increase its market share. This may suggest need for improvement in operation. Above average margins may represent sign of good management, although unusually high margin may attract competitions who may wish to join the scramble for high returns on investment.

PKZ Ltd:

2010: $\dfrac{2{,}640}{12{,}000} \times 100\% = 22\%$

2011: $\dfrac{2{,}940}{14{,}000} \times 100\% = 21\%$

The reduction from 22% t0 21% appears small, but the effect is to reduce gross and net profit by 1% of CU14,000,000 (i.e. CU140,000. The reason for the reduction is implied by the note 2 to the financial statements which stated that the product range and buying price were unchanged over the period under reference.

3.7.3 Trading/Operating Profit Margin - This is given as:

$$\frac{\text{Trading/Operating Profit}}{\text{Turnover}} \times 100\%$$

Trading profit is affected by many more factors than the gross profit, some of which are opened to subjective judgement, such as depreciation and amortisation costs. Inter-company comparisons therefore should be made after suitable adjustments following reconciliation of the accounting policies.

PKZ Ltd:

2010: $\dfrac{690}{12{,}000} \times 100\% = 5.75\%$

2011: $\dfrac{870}{14{,}000} \times 100\% = 6.21\%$

There was a small increase in the net profit % (0.46%), though less than what should have taken place considering the fact that sales increased by one-sixth (2,000/12,000) and expenses debited to the profit and loss account were kept under tight control. The main problem is the decline in the gross profit margin, since this caused the gross as well as the net profit to be about CU140,000 lower than would have been the case if the 22% margin achieved in the year 2010 had been maintained in 2011.

3.7.4 Stock Turnover (i) - This is given as: $\dfrac{\text{Cost of Sales}}{\text{Stocks}} = $ times
(The number of times it takes stock to per annum reach the level of sales)

OR

Stock turnover period (ii) – given as: $\dfrac{\text{Stocks}}{\text{Cost of Sales}} \times 365 \text{ days}$
(How long stocks of goods are kept in inventory)

Sometimes, the computation is based on the average stock (opening stock + closing stock divided by 2). This helps to even the effect of any major change during the period under review. An increasing stock turnover may be an indication some operational difficulty. An increasing number of days or a reducing multiple may indicate that stock is turning over less quickly. This is usually not a good sign as it may reflect lack of demand for the products, poor stock control (with the associated costs such as insurance and storage costs), and may eventually lead to obsolete stocks and stock write-offs. However, it may also be that management are stocking the store in order to take advantage of trade discount, or to avoid stock-outs, or the increase may be due to distortion of ratio caused by comparing a period end stock figure with cost of sales for a period of expansion.

Stock turnover ratios vary considerably with the nature of the business. And companies should consider the reliability of suppliers and the demand for the goods when determining the level of stock holding.

PKZ Ltd:

2010 (i): $\dfrac{9{,}360}{\{1/2(2{,}680 + 2{,}720)\}}$ times = $\dfrac{9{,}360}{2{,}700}$ = 3.47 times

2011 (i): $\dfrac{11{,}060}{\{1/2(2{,}720 + 3{,}000)\}}$ times = $\dfrac{11{,}060}{2{,}860}$ = 3.87 times.

2010 (ii): $\dfrac{\{1/2(2{,}680 + 2{,}720)\}}{9{,}360} \times 365$ days = $\dfrac{2{,}700}{9{,}360} \times 365$ = 105 days.

2011 (ii): $\dfrac{\{1/2(2{,}680 + 3{,}000)\}}{11{,}060} \times 365$ days = $\dfrac{2{,}860}{11{,}060} \times 365$ days = 94 days

There is a significant reduction in the average period for which stocks are held (from 105 to 94 days), and this suggests that management has streamlined the purchasing, selling and distribution functions. Comparing the two balance sheets, it is revealed that the stocks level had increased, but this is expected as there has been a major increase in the level of sales during the year.

3.7.5 Debtors Turnover –
(Rate of debtors' collection)

(i) This is given as:

$$\frac{\text{Trade Debtors}}{\text{Turnover}} \times 100\%$$

OR

Debtors Turnover – (ii) -
(The average length of time it takes customers to pay):

$$\frac{\text{Average Trade Debtors}}{\text{Credit sales/turnover}} \times 365 \text{ days}$$

The trade debtors used in the computation may be a period-end figure or the average for the period. If an average is used to compute the number of days, the ratio obtained is the average number of days' credit taken by the customers. Note that for cash-based businesses such as supermarkets, the debtors' days is not likely to exceed one (1) as there are no real credit sales.

The debtors' turnover should be compared with the company's stated credit policy or credit terms.

A rise in the debtors' days usually suggests absence of proper credit control. It may also be as a result of a deliberate policy to extend the credit period in order attract more customs, or one or two new customers are allowed a different credit terms.

Falling debtors' day, though usually a good sign, could indicate that the company is suffering from lack of adequate cash.

Note that the debtors' days' ratio could be distorted by: using end of period figures which do not represent average debtors, or debt factoring which results in low debtors' level, or other credit finance agreement such as hire purchase, where there is insufficient analysis of turnover to compute proper ratios.

PKZ Ltd:

2010
$$\frac{\{1/2(1,600 + 1,920)\}}{11,000} \times 365 = \frac{1,760}{11,000} \times 365 = 58 \text{ days}$$

2011:
$$\frac{\{1/2(1,920 + 3,120)\}}{13,200} \times 365 = \frac{2,520}{13,200} \times 365 = 70 \text{ days}$$

PKZ Ltd takes an average of over one week (12 days) longer to collect its debts in 2011. This means that a disproportionate amount of fund is tied up in trade debts. These funds are not yielding any return and may be losing value to the business in time of inflation. The reason for this situation requires investigation as it may be a conscious effort on the part of management to maintain attractive positioning of its products. It could also be due to inappropriate or inefficiency of the credit control measures operating in the company.

3.7.6 Creditors Turnover (days) - Rate of payment of creditors/ credit period taken by the suppliers – This is given as:

$$\frac{\text{Trade Creditors}}{\text{Purchases}} \times 365 \text{ days}$$

Average of the trade creditors may also be used in the calculation (i.e. opening creditors + closing creditors divided by 2). If purchases are not known, the cost of sales may be used, otherwise, sales.

The ratio is compared with that of the previous period, together with the company target as stated in its policy. A long credit period may be considered good as it generally indicates a source of free funding for the business; it may also indicate that the company is finding it difficult to pay off its debts more quickly due to liquidity problems. It is important to remember that if the credit period is long, the company may create a negative reputation as a poor payer and may find it difficult to attract new suppliers; even existing suppliers may decide to stop supplies to it; and the company may be losing out in great deals and cash discounts.

PKZ Ltd: We were not given the opening trade creditors for the year 2010. So, we cannot make the calculation based on average creditors' balance. Calculation for 2011 can be made, but as there are no comparative figures, this ratio has very limited interpretative value. However, basing each year's calculation on the closing trade creditors, we could obtain the approximate number of days' purchases represented by the closing balance of the trade creditors. Of course, this does not mean that a similar credit period was obtained throughout the year, unless purchases were made at a uniform rate.

2010: $\quad \dfrac{780}{9{,}400} \times 365 = 30 \text{ days}$

2011: $\dfrac{980}{11{,}340} \times 365 = 31.5$ days

A change in the rate of payment to suppliers may well reflect an improvement or decline in the company's liquidity. Using other ratios to support the position, management is always to ensure that prompt action is taken to arrange for additional funding, otherwise, suppliers may be discouraged from doing more businesses with the company.

3.7.7 Net Assets per share - This gives the rate of utility achieved by the equity holding per unit of monetary currency invested in the net assets and it is given as:

$$\dfrac{\text{Net assets}}{\text{Amount of equity shares in issue.}} : 1$$

3.7.8 Fixed Asset turnover Ratio – Shows the amount of sales/turnover achieved per unit of monetary currency invested in fixed assets; it is an efficiency ratio and it is given as:

$$\dfrac{\text{Turnover}}{\text{Average Fixed Assets}} : 1$$

3.7.9 Total Assets Turnover – This measures the utilisation of the total resources available to management by expressing the amount of turnover achieved per unit of monetary currency invested in gross assets; it is also an efficiency ratio given as:

$$\dfrac{\text{Turnover}}{\text{Average Total Assets}} : 1$$

A high ratio indicates that management is using the assets effectively to generate sales; most probably the company is working at near-full capacity. A decline in the ratio suggests that assets are underutilized and should either be used more fully or sold.

PKZ Ltd

2010: $\dfrac{12{,}000}{\frac{1}{2}(5{,}420 + 5{,}780)} : 1 = \dfrac{12{,}000}{5{,}600} : 1 = 2.14:1$

2011: $\dfrac{14{,}000}{\frac{1}{2}(7{,}380^* + 7{,}790)} : 1 = \dfrac{14{,}000}{7{,}585} : 1 = 1.85:1$

Note* that asset at the end of 2010 totalled CU5,780,000, but cash of CU1,600,000 was received from the debenture issue made on 1 January 2011. This is included in the opening balance for the purpose of computing average total assets during the year 2011.

The ratio may be expressed either as shown above or as an amount of sales per CU1 invested, i.e. sales were CU2.14 per CU1 invested in the year 2010 and CU1.85 per CU1 invested in the year 2011. It is clear that a major reduction in asset utilisation has taken place, principally due to the much longer period of credit extended to the customers in 2011.

3.7.10 The Du-Pont formula and analysis shows that the rate of return on gross assets is the product of total asset turnover and the net profit percentage, i.e.

Secondary Ratios		**Primary Ratio**
Total asset turnover x Net Profit %	=	Rate of return on gross assets

PKZ Ltd:

2010:	2.14 x 5.75%	=	12.31%
2011:	1.85 x 6.20%	=	11.47%

And for equity holders, the key metric of interest is: Return on Equity, given as:

Return on Equity = Operating efficiency x Asset use efficiency x Financial leverage

ROE = Profit margin x Asset turnover x Financial leverage

$$= \frac{\text{Net profit}}{\text{Sales}} \times \frac{\text{Sales}}{\text{Assets}} \times \frac{\text{Assets}}{\text{Equity}}$$

$$= \frac{\text{Net Income *}}{\text{Shareholders' Equity}}$$

Note*: the ratio may be computed on either a pre- or post-tax basis. Whichever basis is used, any preference dividends payable must be deducted since they reduce profits available for ordinary shareholders. Using post-tax basis implies the recognition of the fact that corporation tax must be deducted to arrive at the balance available for distribution to the shareholders.

PKZ Ltd

Pre-tax

2010: $\dfrac{690,000}{½(4,310,000 + 4,500,000)} \times 100\% = 15.66\%$

2011: $\dfrac{710,000}{½(4,500,000 + 4,700,000)} \times 100\% = 15.43\%$

Post-tax

2010: $\dfrac{345,000}{½(4,310,000 + 4,500,000)} \times 100\% = 7.83\%$

2011: $\dfrac{355,000}{½(4,500,000 + 4,700,000)} \times 100\% = 7.5\%$

There was a modest decline in the return earned for the shareholders, but rather less than might have been expected in view of the fairly sharp decline in the primary ratio from 12.31% to 11.50%. The reason for the difference could be that the return earned for shareholders is dependent on three main factors, namely: profit margin, asset utilisation, and the capital structure, business financed significantly by the shareholders.

3.7.11 Note that:

(1) ROCE, once calculated, should be compared with: (a) the previous years' figures and company's target ROCE – provided that there are no changes in accounting policies, or necessary adjustments have been made to aid comparison, otherwise, note the impact of not replacing fixed assets which is that their value will reduce and ROCE will increase; (b) the cost of borrowing – if the cost of borrowing is say 8% and ROCE is 6%, then any additional borrowings will reduce the EPS, except the additional borrowing can be used in areas where the ROCE is higher than the cost of borrowing; and (c) other companies in the same industry – here, care is required in interpretation as there may be different accounting policies used in say: stock valuation, depreciation and research and development, and the different ages of plant and equipment - where assets are written down to low book values, the ROCE will seem to be high, and there may be less assets appearing in the balance sheet such as assets held under finance leases which would appear on the balance sheet while those held under operating lease would not be reflected in line with SSAP 21. If a company had an upward revaluation of fixed assets for instance, this will reduce the ROCE by increasing the capital employed, and decreasing profit by a higher depreciation charge.

In handling associates and investments, note that where the profits excludes investment income, the values for associates and investments should also be excluded from the carrying amounts of capital employed in the balance sheet. This reflects a better measure of operating performance. If associates and investments are not excluded, the total profit figure should include income from investments and associates.

Purchased goodwill may be a subject of amortisation for a long time. This may be eliminated by some analysts before carrying out any detailed analysis.

(2) A company may have a higher profit margin but may be generating less sales per each unit of monetary currency (i.e. under a premium strategy).
(3) Notwithstanding the financing decisions, a company may be performing better if it tends towards a higher ROA (Return on Assets)
(4) Companies with higher asset turnover may be able to generate greater sales for each unit of monetary currency even though they may have lower profit margin (i.e. volume strategy).

3.8 Financial Stability Ratios - calculations

3.8.1 Current or Working Capital Ratio

This measures the adequacy of current assets in meeting the company's short term liabilities and it is given as:

$$\frac{\text{Current Assets}}{\text{Current Liabilities}} : 1$$

A current ratio of 2 or higher was considered adequate for most businesses. More recently, a figure of 1.5 is regarded as normal. A higher figure should be held with suspicion as it may be as a result of high levels of stocks and debtors, or high cash balances which could be better put in more profitable ventures.

Current ratio should be evaluated in the light of what is normal in the type of business. An instance is the supermarkets which tend to have low current ratios due to the fact that they do not have trade debtors, and there is usually very tight cash control.

Consideration should also be given to how easy it is to raise necessary finance (say availability of bank overdraft), the seasonal nature of the business, the level of the long-term liabilities resulting from how they are financed, and the nature of the stock (slow moving of fast moving.)

PKZ Ltd

2010: $\frac{4,680}{1,280} : 1 = 3.66 : 1$

2011: $\frac{6,360}{1,490} : 1 = 4.27 : 1$

A ratio of about 1.5:1 is quite common and so the calculated figures for PKZ Ltd show that the company is financially stable. However, the high ratio may have unfavourable implication for its profitability since resources unnecessarily tied in stock, cash and debtors are not earning any return for the company.

3.8.2 Liquidity (Acid Test or Quick Ratio)

Indicates whether the company has sufficient resources to settle its liabilities and it is given as:

$$\frac{\text{Current Assets} - \text{Stock}}{\text{Current Liabilities}} : 1$$

Generally, the norm for this ratio is 1: 0.7. A higher ratio indicates a more stable option and a strong financial stability. Like the current ratio, it is necessary to the nature of the business in determining the adequacy or otherwise of the ratio.

Sometimes, the quick ratio is computed on the basis of a six-week time frame – quick assets being defined as those which can be turned into cash within six weeks, and quick liabilities as those which must be paid within six weeks. On this basis, quick assets will include bank, cash and short-term investments, and trade debtors; and quick liabilities will be bank overdraft payable on demand, trade creditors, tax and proposed dividends. Company tax liabilities may be excluded.

Note that both the current ratio and quick ratio can be distorted by window dressing, e.g. by paying off a major chunk of the creditors just before the period end out of positive cash balances, thus improving the ratios.

PKZ Ltd

2010: $\dfrac{1,960}{1,280} : 1 = 1.53:1$

2011: $\dfrac{3,360}{1,490} : 1 = 2.26:1$

A liquidity of 1: 1 is desirable, but 1: 0.7 is normal. A ration significantly below this usually causes a company to encounter great difficulty in meeting its debts as they fall due, while in excess of this indicates that the company is in possession of cash resources surplus to requirements. PKZ Ltd's ratios are more than adequate. While there is\ no doubt that the company is solvent, there must be some doubt about it making the best use of the available resources.

3.8.3 Gearing/Leverage Ratio - Gearing is the relationship between a company's equity capital and reserves and its fixed return capital (loans). A company has high gearing when a high proportion of its capital is in the form of preference shares, debentures or loan stock. A company has low gearing if only a small proportion of its capital is in the form of preference shares, debentures or loan stock. A company financed entirely with equity shares has no gearing. The share price of a highly geared company will often be more volatile than that of a company with lower gearing and its earnings are more sensitive to profit changes. And the companies that are better off with high gearing are those with stable profits and assets to use as collateral – such as those in property investment and hotel/leisure services industry. On the other hand, those companies in the extractive trade and high-tech industries where constant changes occur are not generally suitable for high gearing. They generally have insufficient assets to use as collateral.

The objective of companies is to obtain positive leverage – i.e. that the company raises funds at relatively low fixed servicing cost (in terms of interest and dividends) and uses these funds to earn a much higher return than the servicing cost. Known as trading on the equity, this strategy is evidenced by the improvement in earnings per share.

A gearing ratio in excess of 0.6:1 is said to be relatively high, and that below 0.6:1 to be relatively low.

The two methods commonly used to indicate gearing are:

(a) Debt/Equity Ratio, expressed as:

$$\frac{\text{Loans + Preference Share Capital}}{\text{Ordinary shares + Reserves + Minority interest}}$$

OR

$$\frac{\text{Non-current Liabilities}}{\text{Equity}}$$

(b) Percentage of capital employed represented by borrowings, i.e. using total capital as loans, preference share capital, ordinary share capital, reserves and minority interest.

3.8.4 Example

JB Ltd and TY Ltd are established companies. They are engaged in a similar business. Trading conditions changed significantly from year to year, and an analysis of past results achieved by companies in the same line of business show that operating profit before deducting interest charges can fluctuate up to 50% above or below the following estimated results for the forthcoming year.

	JB Ltd CU'000	TY Ltd CU'000
Ordinary share capital (CU1.00 per share) at 1 June 2010	3,000	6,400
Revaluation surplus at 1 June 2010	1,000	2,000
Capital redemption reserve at 1 June 2010	-	1,600
14% Debentures at 1 June 2010	8,000	2,000
Operating profit before interest 2010/2011	1,680	1,680

It is the policy of each company to pay out its entire profits in the form of dividends.

Required:
1. For each company, calculate (a) the estimated rate of return on shareholders' equity; (b) the gearing (i.e. Debt: Equity) ratio
2. Comment on the relative merits of the capital structures of each of the two companies from the shareholders' point of view. Include calculations of maximum possible variations in the return on shareholders' equity.

Answer
1 (a) Estimated Returns on Shareholders' Equity

	JB Ltd CU'000	TY Ltd CU'000
Operating profit	1,680	1,680
Interest charge	1,120	280
Net profit	560	1,400

Equity	(3,000 + 1000)	4,000	
	(6,400+2,000+1,600)		10,000

Return on shareholders' equity: (560/4,000 x 100%) 14%
(1,400/10,000 x 100%) 14%

1 (b) **Debt: Equity** (8,000 : 4,000) = 2 : 1 (2,000 : 10,000) = 1:5

2. Comments

	JB Ltd		TY Ltd	
	+50%	-50%	+50%	-50%
	CU'000	CU'000	CU'000	CU'000
Operating profit	2,520	840	2,520	840
Interest charge	1,120	1,120	280	280
	1,400	(280)	2,240	560
Ordinary share capital	3,000		6,400	
Revaluation surplus	1,000		2,000	
Capital redemption reserve	-		1,600	
Equity	4,000	4,000	10,000	10,000
Return on shareholders' equity	35%	(7%)	22.4%	5.6%

(a) The capital structure of JB Ltd is highly geared. This means that there is a high ratio of debt to equity finance.

(b) The major advantage of gearing is that the return to shareholders will be jacked up when there is a rise in profit – as the additional profit will accrue to the equity shareholders.

(c) This is illustrated above as the increase in profit of 50% raised the return on shareholders' equity to 35% from 14% (by 150%).

(d) On the other hand, when profits decline, the return on equity declines very fast as a result of the fact that the fixed interest charges must still be paid (for JB Ltd: CU1,120

(e) A fall in operating profit of 50% results in a figure for operating profit which is not enough to cover the interest charges and there is a reduction in shareholders' equity to the tune of CU280,000.

(f) The capital structure of TY Ltd is low geared, with debt: equity ratio of 1:5.

(g) A 50% increase in profits results in an increase in the return on shareholders' equity, but the rise is higher to 22.4%.

(h) Conversely, a fall in profits is not so negative to the equity shareholders who continued to receive a return of 5.6% on their investment.

(i) Additional disadvantage of a highly geared company is that it may face acute financial difficulty if there is a major fall in profits. Whereas dividends can be reduced when profits are low, if necessary to a zero level, the accrued interest charges are legal obligations which must be paid irrespective of the level of profits made.

PKZ Ltd:

2010: Zero gearing – no loans, no preference shares.

2011: $\dfrac{1,600}{4,700} : 1 = 0.34 : 1$

A major element of gearing was introduced in 2011 by the issue of an CU1,600,000 debenture to finance an expansion of operations. The policy was not fully successful and the rate of return on total assets declined from 12.31% to 11.50%. However, the shareholders return suffered a moderate decline, and this suggests that, assuming the year 2010's results would otherwise have been repeated, the additional activity produced a return only marginally below the 10% interest payable on the debenture.

3.8.5 Interest Cover - This ratio indicates the cover or security for the interest payable and it is given as:

$$\dfrac{\text{Net Profit before interest and tax}}{\text{Interest Payable}} \text{ times}$$

To calculate the interest cover ratio, use the finance costs line item in the group income statements to represent interest expense for the period. A relatively higher interest coverage ratio reflects positively on the ability of the company to meet its interest obligation from operating income.

PKZ Ltd:
2010: No interest charged.

2011: $\dfrac{870}{160} = 5.43$ times.

This cover appears adequate for the company.

3.8.6 Proprietary Ratio - Indicates the degree to which unsecured creditors are protected against loss in the event of liquidation; it expresses the shareholders' investment, or equity, in the company as a percentage of total sources of finance/total assets. This ratio normally expressed as a percentage is a measure of financial stability, since the larger the proportion of business activity financed by shareholders, the smaller are the creditors' claim against the company. The computation is given as:

$$\frac{\text{Shareholders' Funds}}{\text{Total sources of finance/Total Assets}} \times 100\%$$

PKZ Ltd:

2010: $\dfrac{4{,}500}{4{,}500 + 1{,}280} \times 100\% = \dfrac{4{,}500}{5{,}780} \times 100\% = 77.85\%$

2011: $\dfrac{4{,}700}{4{,}700 + 1{,}600 + 1{,}490} \times 100\% = \dfrac{4{,}700}{7{,}790} \times 100\% = 60.33\%$

The shareholders in PKZ Ltd provided a healthy 78% of total finance at the end of the year 2010, but there is a decline to 60% at the end of the year 2011. The reason for this change is the debenture issued that had a major effect on the financial structure of the company. The shareholders remained the major sources of finance but there is now an increased need to to seek external finance and a corresponding need to meet the yearly interest payments.

Note:
When assessing long-term financial stability, financial balance and overtrading should be considered. Overtrading arises where a company expands its turnover fairly rapidly without securing additional long-term capital adequate for its needs, with the symptoms as: stock increasing, possibly more than proportionately to sales; debtors increasing, possibly more than proportionately to sales; cash and liquid assets declining at a fairly alarming rate; and creditors increasing rapidly.

3.9 Financial Investment (Investors') Ratios - calculations
3.9.1 Earnings per Share (EPS) – This is a primary profitability measure. An increasing EPS is a good sign of a well-managed and profitable business. Earnings per share is the net profit or loss for the period attributable to ordinary shareholders divided by the weighted average number of ordinary shares outstanding during the period. That is, EPS =

Earnings/Net profit or loss for the period attributable to ordinary shareholders
―――
Weighted average number of ordinary shares outstanding in the period

The net profit or loss attributable to ordinary shareholders is the net profit or loss after deducting preference dividends and other appropriations in respect of preference shares.

Both extraordinary and exceptional items are taken into account when determination the EPS (though, in most cases, it is difficult to determine what is extraordinary in business operations). The reason is to help avoid managers hiding under them to paint a better picture of bad result. The EPS may fluctuate from year to year due to the impact of such exceptional items. Therefore, companies are allowed in addition to present alternative measures of EPS. This alternative measure which is likely to be based on profit before exceptional items, especially when the exceptional item is a loss, must be given prominence no greater than the compulsory figure and must be accompanied by a reconciliation and explanation of the adjustments.

3.9.2 If for instance, a company CY Ltd provided the following information for the year 2011:

	CU'000	CU'000
Profit before taxation		600,000
Tax at 30%		180,000
		420,000
Dividends:		
Ordinary shares	200,000	
Preference shares	70,000	270,000
Retained profit		150,000

The company has in issue CU2,000,000 ordinary shares of CU0.50 each and CU100,000 7% preference shares.

Required: To calculate the EPS for 2011.

Answer:
CY Ltd: Calculation of EPS for 2011

$$EPS = \frac{(CU420,000 - 70,000)}{CU2,000,000 \times 2} \times 100 = 8.75$$

Assuming for CY Ltd there was a further issue of 1,200,000 ordinary shares on May 1, 2012, with profit after tax for the year being CU560,000. Then the EPS for 2012 will be:

$$\frac{(560,000 - 70,000)}{(2,000,000 \times 2) + (1,200,000 \times 2/3^*)} \times 100 = \frac{490,000}{4,800,000} \times 100 = 10.21$$

Note* the additional shares issued would enjoy the profit for eight months from May 1 to December 31.

Assume again that for CY Ltd, the result was the same for the year 2011, but during the year 2012, the company made a bonus issue of one additional share for every two shares presently held and the profit after tax for 2012 were CU500,000.

Required:
1. Calculate the EPS for 2012; and
2. Calculate the revised EPS for 2011.

Answer

CY Ltd: Calculation of EPS

2012:
$$\frac{(CU500,000 - CU70,000)}{(CU2,000,000 \times 2) + \{(2,000,000 \times 2)/2\}} \times 100 = \frac{430,000}{6,000,000} \times 100 = 7.17$$

2011:
$$\frac{CU420,000 - CU70,000)}{(CU2,000,000 \times 2) + \{2,000,000 \times 2)/2\}} \times 100 = \frac{350,000}{6,000,000} \times 100 = 5.83$$

The result adjusts for the fact that there were 50% more shares in issue in 2012 compared with 2011.

If there is a rights issue, the market price of the share should fall. Rights issue occurs when new shares are issued to existing shareholders, usually at below the existing market price. This increases the number of shares in issue, but does not increase the earning capacity of the company proportionately.

3.9.3 Illustrating this, assume:
Eight shares in circulation before rights issue at a market price of CU2.00 each = CU16. Rights issue of say one for two at the price of CU0.50 each (i.e. 4 shares)   =

                                                                               2

Then twelve shares in issue will have a theoretical low price of   18

Theoretical ex-rights price will be CU18/12shares   1.50

Diluted post-rights equivalent of pre-rights issue shares:

8 shares worth CU2.00 each (pre-issue) will be 10.67 shares - post issue
{i.e. 8 x (CU2.00/1.50)}

Proof:

Eight shares at pre-issue market price of CU2.00 each = CU16.00
10.67 shares at theoretical ex-rights price of CU1.50   = CU 16.00

These adjustments are used in the calculation of EPS in the following manner:

1. Calculate total value of equity before rights issue - market price x number of shares.
2. Calculate proceeds of new issue.
3. Calculate theoretical price after issue, which is:

$$\frac{1 + 2}{\text{Number of shares after rights issue}}$$

4. Calculate the post-issue equivalent of number of shares outstanding pre-issue, i.e.

$$\text{Number of shares} \times \frac{\text{Actual pre-issue price}}{\text{Theoretical post-issue price}}$$

5. Calculate the number of shares in issue during the year on the weighted average basis.
6. Compute the EPS.
7. Obtain corresponding comparative figure for previous year, i.e.

$$\text{Previous year's EPS} \times \frac{\text{Theoretical post-issue price}}{\text{Actual pre-issue price}}$$

3.9.4 Example:

The following information is provided for KKP Ltd:

- KKP Ltd has earnings of CU33, 280 for the year 2011.
- There were 240,000 ordinary shares in issue at the start of the year.
- 80,000 further shares were issued on 31 August 2011 at the price of CU1.50 each.
- The market price of each share immediately before the rights issue was CU2.00.

Required:

Calculate the EPS for 2011.

Answer:

How to calculate the EPS:
1. Calculate the total value of equity before issue, i.e. market price x number of shares: = CU2.00 x 240,000 = CU480,000.
2. Calculate the proceeds of new issue, i.e. CU1.50 x 80,000 = CU120,000
3. Calculate the theoretical price after the issue, i.e.

$$\frac{CU480{,}000 + CU120{,}000}{240{,}000 + 80{,}000} = \frac{600{,}000}{320{,}000} = CU1.875$$

4. Calculate the post-issue equivalent of the number of shares outstanding pre-issue:

$$240{,}000 \times \frac{CU2.00}{CU1.875} = 256{,}000 \text{ shares.}$$

5. Calculate the number of shares in issue during the year on the weighted average basis:

$$(256{,}000 \times 8/12) + \{(240{,}000 + 80{,}000) \times 4/12\}$$

$$170{,}667 + 106{,}667 = 277{,}334 \text{ shares}$$

6. Compute the EPS: $\dfrac{CU33{,}280}{277{,}334} \times 100 = 12.00$

3.9.5 Limitations in the use of EPS

Generally, the stock market places great emphasis on a company's P/E ratio. Therefore, a standard form of measuring EPS is required. The trend in EPS may be a more accurate performance indicator than the trend in profit. However, the use of EPS is subject to some limitations.

1. Where there has been an issue of shares during the period, these are normally included in the weighted average number of shares. This is done on the basis that earnings will also immediately increase as a result of the income generated from the new project financed with the issuance of shares. But in practice, this may not be so. Accordingly, the issuance of shares is generally accompanied with a reduction in EPS calculated. Where there is an issue of shares at full market price during the period, use the earnings figure for the period without adjustment, but divide by the average number of shares weighted on a time basis.
2. EPS is dependent on earnings figure which is a subjective computation. Some of the elements of those earnings are subjective, such as movements in provisions and some are affected by the policy as defined by individual management such as the depreciation rates applied.
3. In times of rising prices, the EPS will increase as profits increase. It is therefore suggested that any increase in the EPS should be considered in the light of the effect of price level changes on the business profits.
4. EPS is a historical figure and based on past accounts; it does not take account of inflation, and being based on historical information, does not necessarily have predictive value. This is not supportive to the use of a futuristic figure such as the price-earnings ratio.

5. EPS cannot be used as a basis of comparison between two companies as the number of shares in issue in a particular company is not related to the amount of capital employed. An example is where a company has 200,000 CU1 shares in issue and reserves of CU560,000, and another has two million CU0.50 shares in issue and reserves of CU600,000. Even though they have the same earnings, they will have different EPS figures.

6. It is far too simple to just take one earnings figure and use it as a key performance measure in performance analysis. And FRS 3 has emphasised this limitation in interpreting and comparing financial statements.

3.9. 6 Price Earnings Ratio (P/E Ratio)

The figure, earnings per share (EPS), is used to compute the major stock market indicator of performance, the Price Earnings Ratio (PE ratio). Price/Earnings Ratio is the stock market measure that is most widely referred to. It is also commonly referred to as an earnings multiple. The higher the P/E ratio, the faster the growth the market is expecting in the company's future EPS. It is computed as the purchase of a number of years' earnings, and represents the market's consensus of the future prospects of that share. P/E Ratio =

$$\frac{\text{Market price (value) per share}}{\text{Earnings per share (EPS)}}$$

3.9.7 Dividend Yield – This is the percentage of the dividend (grossed up) to the market price, indicating the current return on investment, and it is given as:

$$\frac{\text{Gross Dividend Per Share}}{\text{Market Price per Share}} \times 100\%$$

The dividends are grossed up in order to show the total amount including the tax credit. Thus, at the tax rate of 10%, the amount of dividend per share will be equal to 10/90 of that net amount received.

3.9.8 Dividend Cover – This is the relationship between the profits, adjusted to exclude non-trading profits and losses, and the dividends pay out of the profits. It is given as:

$$\frac{\text{Profits (net of non-trading profits)}}{\text{Dividends paid}} \text{ times}$$

The higher the dividends cover, the more likely it is that the current dividend level can be sustained in the future.

3.10 Working Capital Cycle, Ratios and Considerations

3.10.1 Working Capital describes the account balances used in the day to day trading. The working capital cycle is an indicator of a company's liquidity and day to day cash flow management (operating cash needs).

3.10.2 The Working Capital Cycle:

| Raw Materials in Stock | → | Period of credit taken from Suppliers | → | Time taken to produce to goods | → | Finished goods in stock | → | Time taken by customers to pay for goods |

Length of Working Capital Cycle = X days **minus** X days **plus** X days **plus** X days **plus** X days

In addition to the current ratio and the quick ratio, which give an understanding of a company's overall liquidity, the following measures can be used to gain understanding of the length of the different parts of the working capital cycle:

3.10.3 Payables turnover period – The average length of time to pay suppliers for items bought on credit.

$$\frac{\text{Average trade Payables/creditors}}{\text{Purchases on credit terms for a year}} \times 365 \text{ days}$$

3.10.4 Inventory/Stock turnover period – How long goods are kept in stock.

$$\frac{\text{Inventory/stock Value}}{\text{Cost of Sales}} \times 365 \text{ days}$$

A relatively lower inventory turnover period may suggest less operating cash tied up in the context of sales activity.

3.10.5 Receivable/Debtors turnover period – This shows the average length of time it takes the customers to pay what they owe, and it is given as:

$$\frac{\text{Average trade receivables}}{\text{Credit sales for the year}} \times 365 \text{ days}$$

3.10.6 Working Capital Considerations

Within the industry competition and the traditional strategic and decision making frameworks, the effects of the five common drivers of working capital on assets and liabilities must be considered:

- Threat of new entrants into the industry - Volume and value of sales and by extension receivables may depend on the success or otherwise of new entrants.
- Threat of substitutes for the goods - Success of new substitutes may significantly influence the decision of both the customers and suppliers.
- Bargaining power of customers – The receivables period may depend on the bargaining power of customers.
- Bargaining power of Suppliers – Credit terms offered by suppliers may depend on demand and supply.
- Competitive Rivalry – This can increase both the bargaining power of suppliers and customers by having a magnifying impact on their influence.

Note:
- Financial ratios are useful tools in identifying major relationships between different figures in the financial statements. But they should not be read in isolation. It is necessary to consider them in relation to other available information about the company. Such include, among others:

(i) The approved budget figures.
(ii) The industrial average.
(iii) The ideal/attainable figures.
(iv) Comparable figures from similar businesses.
(v) Comparable figures from the same businesses.

3.11 Limitations of Financial Ratios

Irrespective of the general utility of ratios, they still have some basic limitations, amongst which are:

(1) Different business entities may adapt different accounting policies and may also use different methods in accounting for certain accounting items, thereby producing different figures making comparisons inappropriate (e.g. accounting periods covered, the methods used by entities to account for tangible fixed assets, stocks, development expenditure, and leases can affect ROCE, gearing and profits.)

(2) Ratios based on current cost accounts (CCA) may provide more useful information than those based on historic cost accounts (HCA).

(3) Though there are general guidelines, for instance, that the quick ratio should not be less than 1, there is no such thing as an "ideal" ratio. A quick ratio of less than 1 may be acceptable in some businesses, but may not be very low for another.

(4) Unless ratios are calculated on a uniform basis and from a uniform data, any comparisons may be inappropriate and misleading. In comparing company ratios, care must be taken to ensure that the data is consistent.

(5) Ratios based on current purchasing power accounts (CPPA) may provide more useful information as they adjust for inflation.

(6) Financial statements only reflect activities which can be translated in monetary terms. They therefore do not give the complete picture of the activities of the company – and therefore ratios derived may not give the complete picture and its actual position and financial strength.

(7) Ratios cannot be used as the sole test of company viability and efficiency. Using just a few financial ratios cannot provide a reliable tool for running a company and solving business problems. And relying on a few ratios may inhibit management from taking some risks to expand and grow the business to the detriment of the long-term benefit of the company.

Note:
It is important to be able to prepare and present reports for the different users and purposes. The issue of producing written reports is in the context of inter-company and inter-temporal comparisons, and this is captured in two basic sections, namely:

(a) Main body, including conclusions reached.
(b) Statistical appendices and supplementary statements supporting the comments and conclusions reached.

Practically, however, under exam conditions, the following is a summary of a suitable approach to adopt when setting out the report:

(a) Index to the report.
(b) Addressee, Date, and Title of the report.
(c) Introduction – Introducing the reader to the purpose of the report.
(d) State the main assumptions considered in the report.
(e) Information used – stating the source of the financial information included in the report and the extent to which the report has been limited by specific instructions.
(f) State the conclusions reached as clearly as possible (which may appear

at the very beginning of the report).
(g) Appendices – containing detailed figures as used in the body of the report.

3.12 Trend Analysis

Companies usually include a summary of the results of their operations for the last few years in their financial statements. This assists users in appreciating their overall financial position or strength. It enables the users to appreciate how the company had arrived at the current state of affairs and therefore enable them to look at the current results in the context of the disclosed trend.

Usually, published financial statements give comparative information in:
(a) The related amounts for items included in the balance sheet, profit and loss account, and the notes – in line with the requirements of the Company Act.
(b) Any historical summary provided – such summaries taking the form of five- to ten years details (though not a requirement of any law but just as a common feature with financial statements of quoted companies).

In analysing the trend of any company, it is important to consider any change in its accounting policy during the summary period and also whether the summarised figures have been adjusted for the effects of inflation, and if not, what adjustments are necessary to enable any conclusions to be reached.

3.13 Time Series

The most common measure of trend over multiple time periods is the compound annual growth rate (CAGR).

CAGR can be defined as: "The year-over-year growth rate of an investment over a specified period of time. It can be applied to sales, costs, headcount, and share prices etc – anything for which trend data exists.

The compound annual growth rate is calculated by taking the nth root of the total percentage growth rate, where n is the number of years in the period under consideration.

$$CAGR = \{Ending\ Value / Beginning\ Value\}^{(1/n)} - 1$$

The major advantages of CAGR are that: (i) it is the best formula for evaluating how different investments have performed over time; (ii) investors can compare the CAGR in order to evaluate how well one stock performed against other stocks in a peer group or against a market index.

The major disadvantages are that: (i) it does not take into consideration the investment risk or volatility as it looks at first and last years; (ii) it requires one to ensure the use of the same time periods when comparing the CAGR's of two companies – this can be very difficult if the companies have different year ends.

It is important to note that ratios will be influenced by the type of business carried out; so, there is no universal "good" or "bad" ratio. For example, the following reflect the positions of different companies under different type of businesses, all equally performing well:

	Retail Businesses	Consumer/Professional Services	Engineering & Manufacturing Companies
Asset Turnover	TAB = 1.2 SAB = 1.8 MAB = 1.8	DOT = 2.2 POT = 1.7 KOT = 1.6	SMT = 0.8 CMT = 0.7 BMT = 0.8

Asset turnover here is uniformly low for the strong manufacturing companies and consistently higher for high volume retail businesses.

	Retail Businesses	Consumer/Professional Services	Engineering & Manufacturing Companies
Operating Profit Margin	TAB = 6.2% SAB = 3.5% MAB = 5.2%	DOT = 28.7% POT = 33.5% KOT = 14.6%	SMT = 15.4% CMT = 15.6% BMT = 6.8%
	Low margin, High volume Industry	Limited cost base allows for high margins	High value-added, but significant cost base

Part 4

Reading and Interpretation of Financial Statements
Worked Examples – Questions and Answers

4.1. Reading and Interpreting Financial Statements

When commencing to use financial statements – reading a company's annual reports and the comparative analysis - it may be helpful to consider the following aspects:

(a) Company covered – Is it a group (consolidated) or for a single company.
(b) Reporting date – Is it the end of a calendar year? Or, other period?
(c) Period covered – It is usually 12 months (but sometimes it may not).
(d) Accounting standard employed – Is it the IFRS, US GAAP, IFRS for SMEs?
(e) Currency and units of figures reported – Pound, Dollar, Euro, etc. – in thousands or millions?
(f) Post-balance sheet events reported – the events that occur between the balance sheet date and the date of signing the financial statements that have a material impact on the financial statements.
(g) Auditors' opinion – financial statements should have unqualified opinion that they give a "true and fair view. Qualified opinion means that the auditors were not satisfied with the financial statements.

In comparing financial statements of two different companies, you are to consider:

(a) Whether the companies are similar – Group (consolidated) or single company; is the revenue/business model substantially similar?
(b) Are the reporting period the same? How much do they overlap?
(c) What period is covered? Are the periods of the same length? Otherwise, apply pro-rata basis.
(d) The accounting standards employed – are they the same? If not, will this have a material impact?
(e) Currency and units of presentation – Do you need to convert? If you are, note that the balance sheet items are to be converted at spot rate, while the income statement items are at period average.
(f) The annual report and notes to the accounts – what explains the differences between two or more companies? Are there any one-off items?

4.2. Worked Examples

Question 1: Operating profit is one of the major items in a company's financial statements used in analysing and interpreting its performances. In arriving at this operating profit figure, some elements are included which may affect the analysis.

List some examples of these elements.

Answer 1:
1. Examples include:
(a) Depreciation of assets (tangible assets)
(b) Amortisation of intangible assets.
(c) Exceptional items, e.g. Advertising expenditure
(d) Staff costs – salaries and benefits, e.g. Emoluments paid to directors.
(e) Government grants received.
(f) Research and Development costs; etc.

Question 2: ABC Ltd re-valued its fixed assets during the last accounting period. How will this exercise affect the Return on Capital Employed (ROCE) calculated?

Answer 2. If the fixed assets are re-valued upwards, this will have the effect of lowering the ROCE by: (a) increasing the capital employed, and (b) decreasing the profits by a higher depreciation charge.

Question 3: Two companies Biggy Ltd and City Ltd, both have capital of CU20,000. Biggy Ltd has it all in the form of equity shares of CU1.00 each; City Ltd has 10,000 CU1.00 equity shares and CU10,000 of 10% debentures. The two companies earn operating profits of CU10,000 in the first year and CU4,000 in the second year.
Assume corporate tax of 35%, with dividend paid at CU0.10 per share each year. The capital position is therefore as follows:

	Biggy Ltd	City Ltd
	CU	CU
Shares	20,000	10,000
Debentures	-	10,000
	20,000	20,000

What is the EPS in each year?

Answer 3:

	Biggy Ltd		City Ltd	
	Year 1	Year 2	Year 1	Year 2
	CU	CU	CU	CU
Profit before tax and Debenture interest	10,000	4,000	10,000	4,000
Debenture interest	-	-	1,000	1,000
	10,000	4,000	9,000	3,000
Taxation at 35%	3,500	1,400	3,150	1,050
Earnings	6,500	2,600	5,850	1,950
Dividend at 10%	2,000	2,000	1,000	1,000
Retained profits	4,500	600	4,850	950
EPS: Net Profit/Earnings	6,500	2,600	5,850	1,950
No. of Ord. Shares	20,000	20,000	10,000	10,000
	CU0.325	CU0.13	CU0.585	CU0.195

Comments:
This question shows the effects of gearing in the capital structure of a company. Since debenture interest is tax deductible while dividends are paid after tax is deducted, City Ltd (with debentures in its capital structure) has higher retained earnings than Biggy Ltd. Earnings of a highly geared company are more sensitive to profit changes; therefore, the share price of a highly geared company will often be more volatile than that having a less amount of gearing. So, assuming the investors value their shares by applying a multiple to the earnings per share, known as the P/E ratio, and using a multiple of say, 5 to the EPS calculated above, the share valuations will be as follows:

	Biggy Ltd		City Ltd	
Year	01	02	01	02
Share price (EPS x 5)	CU1.625	CU0.65	CU2.925	CU0.975

But note that for a company to use gearing successfully, it must have at least, two features, namely: relatively consistent profit figures, and suitable fixed assets for use as collateral security for the loans.

Question 4: Can you explain why trends in accounting ratios may provide a more useful insight into the financial position and performance of an entity than the current financial statements considered solely on their own?

Answer 4: Trends in accounting ratios can provide information from which future performance of a company can be predicted. This is particularly so if the figures are very stable and consistent.

Comparative figures for many years give information about the way in which the financial position and performance of a company has changed over the years. If for instance a company has a low liquidity ratio (current ratio and/or quick ratio) for a given year, this would ordinarily indicate liquidity difficulties. But if low ratios are considered in the light of a consistently improving trend, the picture could be different – the company is able to survive at this level, it is solving its liquidity problems, and it is likely to avoid liquidation in the near future.

The level to which financial figures and ratios are stable or volatile can reveal a lot about a company. Unstable ratios, or ratios that are subject to sudden changes in trends, may give away the fact that the company will experience serious difficulties in the future. This is so even if performance appears to be improving.

Question 5: With respect to using financial ratios calculated from company data, what particular problems may arise from the choice of a year end for that company?

Answer 5: An accounting year end is the cut-off date for the production of the financial statements of companies. But the accounting year covered by the financial statements may not reflect a representative financial position of the company. Some companies produce and present accounts to a date on which there is a relatively low level of trading activity. For instance, retail organisations often have an end of March accounting date, a date after the peak of Christmas trading and January and February sales. Following this, the items on the balance sheet are not truly representative of items throughout the accounting year. An example is the stock levels of a retail outfit. They may vary considerably during the year. Adding the opening balance to the closing balance and dividing by two to obtain an average may not generate a fair average.

Question 6: The following five-year summary relates to BFL Ltd, and is based on the financial statements prepared under the historic cost convention.

Year		2012	2011	2010	2009	2008

Financial Ratios:

Profitability –

$$\text{Margin} = \frac{\text{Trading Profit}}{\text{Sales}} \%$$ 7.8 7.5 7.0 7.2 7.3

$$\text{Return on Assets} = \frac{\text{Trading Profit}}{\text{Net Operating Assets}} \%$$ 16.3 17.6 16.2 18.2 18.3

Interest and dividend Cover:

$$\text{Interest Cover} = \frac{\text{Trading Profit}}{\text{Net Finance Charges}} \text{ times}$$ 2.9 4.8 5.1 6.5 3.6

$$\text{Dividend Cover} = \frac{\text{Earnings per Ord. Shares}}{\text{Dividend per Ord. Share}} \text{ times}$$ 2.7 2.6 2.1 2.5 3.1

Debt to Equity Ratios:

$$\frac{\text{Net borrowings}}{\text{Shareholders' funds}} \%$$ 65.9 61.3 48.3 10.8 36.5

$$\frac{\text{Net borrowings}}{\text{Shareholders' funds + Minority interest}} \%$$ 59.3 55.5 44.0 10.1 33.9

Liquidity Ratios:

$$\text{Current} = \frac{\text{Current Assets}}{\text{Current Liabilities}} \%$$ 133.6 130.3 142.2 178.9 174.7

$$\text{Quick} = \frac{\text{Current Assets - Stocks}}{\text{Current Liabilities}} \%\qquad 82.1\quad 81.9\quad 83.4\quad 94.2\quad 101.2$$

Asset Ratios:

$$\frac{\text{Sales}}{\text{Net operating Assets}} \text{ times}\qquad 2.1\quad 2.4\quad 2.3\quad 2.5\quad 2.5$$

$$\frac{\text{Sales}}{\text{Working Capital}} \text{ times}\qquad 8.6\quad 8.0\quad 7.0\quad 7.4\quad 6.2$$

Per Share:

Earnings per share – in Currency Unit (CU)	0.1565	0.1360	0.1098	0.132	0.1218
Dividend per share	0.590	0.540	0.490	0.460	0.410
Net Assets per share	1.0210	0.8922	0.8595	0.8579	0.7811

Net operating assets include tangible assets, stock, debtors and creditors. They exclude borrowings, taxation and dividends.

Required:

Prepare a report on the company, clearly interpreting and evaluating the information provided. Include comments on possible effects of price changes which may limit the quality of the report.

Answer 6:

Note: This is an internal report question on the interpretation of accounts that does not involve the calculation of ratios. You are expected to use the grouping of ratios given as a guide to structure and develop your report. It is important to avoid repeating the data given, and make sensible suggestions, including the need for further information. Your answer must include comments on the effects of changing price levels on a "trend analysis" of this nature. The appendix would contain the details given in the question.

INTERNAL REPORT

To: The Managing Director
From: Peter Duke, Analyst
Date: xx – xx – 20xx

Subject: Interpretation and Evaluation of Five-Year Financial Statement Summary

This report and the comments are based on the financial ratios derived from the analysis of the financial statements of BFL Ltd for the five-year period, 2008 – 2012. The ratios and their method of computation are detailed in the appendix to this report.

Profitability
The amount of trading profit in relation to both sales and operating assets has remained consistent over the five-year period. The profit margin percentage declined in the early years of the period (2009 and 2010), but improved steadily from 2011, reaching the peak in 2012. Management should attempt to find out the reason for this trend – could it be due to the application of a cost saving method, or an increase in selling price? – and try to maintain it. However, the level of profitability is now consuming relatively higher level of net operating assets. It might be necessary for management to endeavour to make optimum use of the assets available, though it is possible that the drop from 2011 to 2012 is the result of the acquisition of new assets which are yet to generate a return.

Interest and Interest Cover
The interest cover has varied over the five-year period. But this does not appear to indicate any specific problem for the company as the interest is sufficiently covered. However, there is a steady decline from 2010, and if this trend continues, the company may find it difficult to raise finance from sources who use such a ratio as an indicator of a company's ability to meet its interest obligations. To such sources, probably of more interest is the cash available to effect such payments, thus making liquidity ratios of more relevance.

The dividend cover shows that in the recent years, 2011 and 2012, the amount of earnings retained in the business for capital maintenance and expansion has increased. This may be as a result of management efficiency, but the level of dividend must be maintained to give the shareholders a fair return on their investment. This would be of special interest to shareholders who invest for periodic income not capital growth.

Debt to Equity Ratios
These ratios are of interest to both lenders and shareholders alike. The two ratios, one with and one without the minority interest as part of the equity, follow the same pattern, and the level of minority interests within the company has therefore remained fairly stable.

Generally referred to as Gearing Ratios, these ratios indicate that the relative amount of long-term finance provided by borrowing is increasing. This may have accounted for the declining interest cover as noted earlier. The level of gearing has become higher, such that over 59% of long-term finance was provided by borrowing in 2012 compared with just about 10% in 2009. This may be as a result of taking advantage of "cheaper" long-term finance, but management need to take care considering the fact that the higher the gearing, the riskier any investment in the company, especially during the period of unstable profitability when fixed interest payments cannot be adjusted in line with the variable profit levels.

Liquidity Ratios
These ratios are important indicators of the short-term profitability of the company. Worthy of note is to remember that companies often go into liquidation because of cash flow difficulties rather than lack of profits. Currently, the company has enough liquid or near liquid assets to meet its immediate liabilities. This may initially be considered as a sign of weakness in the company, but the position having existed since 2008 could now be considered as acceptable level. However, management should ensure that the position does not deteriorate; otherwise, the company may find it difficult to operate in future.

Asset Ratios
Here, the ratio of sales to net operating assets shows a little decline. This could be as a result of increased investment in fixed assets as noted earlier; but it could also be as a result of a declining level of sales. Management should ensure that that any downward trend in real sales level is not allowed to continue.

The sales/working capital ratio shows a fall in the relative value of the working capital. This is connected with the liquidity difficulty, but shows that there could be a better way to use the net current assets.

Per Share
The three ratios indicate an improving position for the earnings, dividends and net assets per share. This may prove to be very useful if future long-term funds are to be requested from the equity investors – new or current shareholders – by way of rights issue. The ratio relating to net assets shows that the company is probably financing additional assets by way of retained profits. The dividends per share have also increased.

In all, the position of the shareholders seems favourable but it is necessary to consider these ratios in the light of the market prices of the shares during the five-year period. This would enable the calculation of the Price/Earnings ratio – considered to be a very useful market indicator. The use of the share price would put these per share ratios into better perspective.

General Conclusion
For some of the issues raised in this report in relation to the ratios, management should consider them in the light of the ratios reported by other similar companies. Participating in an inter-company comparison scheme is recommended. While maintaining non-identification of participants, this scheme enables the comparison of the company's financial ratios with those of others in a similar business and the averages for the industry sector.

The ratios used to generate this report have been calculated using information contained in the financial statements prepared under the historic cost convention. It may be necessary to adjust some of the figures to reflect the price level changes, especially where one figure in the ratio is affected by inflation at different rate to the other figure in the ratio. An example includes some of the assets which may require adjusts by reference to the specific index of price level changes while another would be adjusted using a general price index. And this could significantly affect the trend indicated by a ratio.

Signed: xxxxx

Question 7: Mr. D, Jones inherited a 20% shareholding in a private company, Tonto Ltd. The company manufactures DIY equipment that are sold to retailers and through a cash sales outlet from the company's factory sites.

Mr. D. Jones is not sure whether the company is being well managed and has asked for your assistance in looking at the financial statements. He tells you that the mark-up is usually 100% on cost in the type of business of which about two-thirds goes in overheads. He also informed you that the external liabilities are normally about a quarter of the equity (0.25:1) and that interest normally comprises about 20% of operating profit (5:1).

The following financial information is available:

Profit and Loss Account for the Year Ended 31 December, 2011

	CU'000
Sales	11,000
Cost of sales	5,400
Gross profit	5,600
Administration expenses	750
Distribution costs	2,350
Operating profit	2,500
Interest charges	600
	1,900
Taxation	440
	1,460
Dividend	300
	1,160
Profit brought forward	1,300
	2,460

Balance sheet as at 31 December 2011

	CU'000	CU,000
Fixed asset		12,000
Current assets:		
Stocks	470	
Debtors	470	
Cash	460	
	1,400	
Current liabilities:		
Creditors	610	
Dividends	200	
Taxation	460	
	1,270	
		130
		12,130
Creditors falling due in more than one year:		
Debenture		6,000
		6,130
Share capital and reserves:		
Share capital		3,670
Profit and loss account		2,460
		6,130

Required:
1. Calculate:
a. Three ratios based on the above financial statements which examine the management of working capital.
b. Three ratios based on the above financial statements which examine the profitability of the company.
c. Two ratios based on the above financial statements which examine the capital structure of the company.
Where possible, the ratios calculated should be those in respect of which comparative data is available.

2. Comment on the financial position and performance of Tonto Ltd based on the results of your calculations under (1) and the information provided in the question.

Answer 7:
(a)

(i) Management of working capital ratios:

Ratio	Calculation
Current Or working capital	$\dfrac{\text{Current assets}}{\text{Current liabilities}} = \dfrac{1{,}400}{1{,}270} = 1.1 : 1$
Liquidity	$\dfrac{\text{Current assets - stocks}}{\text{Current liabilities}} = \dfrac{1{,}400 - 470}{1{,}270} = 0.73 : 1$
Debtors' turnover	$\dfrac{\text{Trade debtors}}{\text{Sales}} \times 365 = \dfrac{470}{11{,}000} \times 365 = 15.6 \text{ days}$

(ii). Profitability ratios

Ratio	Calculation
Gross profit percentage	$\dfrac{5{,}600}{11{,}000} \times 100\% = 51\%$
Net operating profit percentage	$\dfrac{2{,}500}{11{,}000} \times 100\% = 22.73\%$
Return on gross assets	$\dfrac{2{,}500}{13{,}400} \times 100\% = 18.66\%$

(iii). Capital structure ratios

Ratios	Calculation
Gearing	$\dfrac{6{,}000}{6{,}000 + 6{,}130} \times 100\% = 49.46\%$
Interest cover	$\dfrac{2{,}500}{600} = 4.17 : 1$

(b). Comments on the financial position and performance of Tonto Ltd

Management of working capital
The current/working capital ratio of 1.1: 1 is not easily interpreted in the absence of comparative figures for a similar company. However, a ratio of 2:1 is usually accepted as the norm for manufacturing companies and Tonto's computed figure would suggest that the company may have difficulty in meeting its short-term liabilities as they fall due.

The liquidity ratio is also below the acceptable industry average of 1: 1. It therefore seems that the company is suffering from liquidity problems and the payment of tax and dividends may result in the need to arrange short term finance such as overdraft (although the cash position reported in the financial statements seems reasonably healthy.)

The rate of debtors' collection seems fast (about 15 days) – a credit period of 30 days is usually the norm. However, an unknown proportion of the sales are made through cash sales outlet from the company factory site. Therefore, a further observation of the efficiency of the collection period is quite difficult.

Profitability
The mark-up, we are told is 100% on cost in the business. This implies a gross profit of 50%. Given that Tonto Ltd has succeeded in generating a gross profit percentage of 51% suggests that the company's margins are in line with industry expectations.

We are told too that a further expectation of two-thirds of the gross profit will be absorbed through overheads. This implies a net profit percentage of 17% (1/3 x 51%). Tonto Ltd achieved a much better result (22.73%) suggesting effective control of overheads and or better asset utilisation.

The return earned on gross asset seems healthy too (18.66%), though it is difficult to draw any firm conclusions regarding its adequacy in view of the fact that the assets are valued at historical cost and there are no comparative figures supplied.

Capital structure ratio

We are told that a normal ratio of external liabilities to equity is 0.25:1. For Tonto Ltd, this figure is 1.2:1. This implies that the company is highly geared compared with the industry norm. It suggests a possibility of financial difficulties if the profits decline but relatively high returns for shareholders in the company when profits are high. This may well explain the apparently healthy return on the shareholders' equity (over 23%).

The interest cover of 4.17:1 is a little below the industry norm. This is the expected consequence of the high level of gearing in the company, though moderated by a relatively healthy level of profitability.

Question 8:

The following information is provided for JJB Ltd and ADK Ltd, which supply a similar range of products but are located in different geographical areas and are not in competition with each other.

	JJB Ltd	ADK Ltd
	CU'000	CU'000
Operating profit	1,200	2,400
Turnover	14,200	18,000
Average investment in gross assets	4,800	12,000

The following accounting ratios are provided by the trade association to which they each belong. The ratios are averages for members of the association.

Gross asset turnover	1.5
Operating profit percentage	14%
Rate of return on gross assets	21%

Required:
(a) Separate calculations for JJB Ltd and ADK Ltd of the accounting ratios equivalent to those provided by the trade association.
(b) An explanation of the relationship between the three ratios and advice about how the relationship might be explored in greater detail.
(c) An analysis of the performance of JJB Ltd and ADK Ltd by comparison with members of the trade association and with each other.

Answer 8:
(a)

	JJB Ltd	ADK Ltd
Gross asset turnover	14,400/4,800 = 3	18,000/12,000 = 1.5
Operating profit %	1,200/14,400 x 100% = 8.33%	2,400/18,000 x 100% = 13.33%
Rate of return on Gross Assets	1,200/4,800 x 100% = 25%	2,400/12,000 x 100% = 20%

(b). The rate of return on gross assets is the product of the operating profit percentage and gross asset turnover. A business organisation may improve its profitability in two main ways, namely: It may either achieve more sales per CU invested or sell its products at a higher margin. The first of these strategies is measured by the gross asset turnover and the second by the operating profit percentage. It is therefore possible for a business to pursue divergent strategies in an effort to maximise the return on shareholders' investment in the company. They might choose to sell their products at low margins with the view to achieving greater asset turnover, or they might set higher prices and accept the fact that the level of sales will be lower and asset utilisation correspondingly reduced.

(c). The typical comment might include the following:
- The directors of ADK Ltd follow business policies that result in a ratio of gross asset turnover in line with that achieved, on average, by members of the trade association. The directors of JJB Ltd have succeeded in achieving twice the level of asset turnover reflecting a much greater ability to make assets work more.
- The operating profit percentage of ADK Ltd is closely in line with the trade association average, indicating a price and cost structure in line with what might be regarded as the typical firm in the industry. The operating profit percentage of JJB Ltd is significantly lower, possibly reflecting a

lower pricing policy designed to increase the level of sales and asset utilisation.
• The rate of return earned by ADK Ltd on gross assets is marginally below that of the average members of the trade association, reflecting the slightly lower operating profit percentage. The rate of return by JJB Ltd is significantly higher, indicating the success of their combined strategy of lower prices and higher asset utilisation compared with the average firm.

Question 9:
The following information is provided in respect of PAC Ltd:
1.
Profit and loss account extracts, year ended 31 December:

	2011	2010
	CU'000	CU'000
Operating profit	264	216
Interest payable	72	72
Profit on ordinary activities	192	144
Taxation	64	48
Profit after taxation	128	96
Dividends – ordinary shares	(64)	(32)
Dividends – Preference shares	(16)	(16)
Retained profits	48	48

2. The ordinary share capital consisted of 60,000 shares of CU1.00 each in 2010 and through 30th April 2011 when a bonus issue was made of five new ordinary shares for every one share presently held.
3. The 8% preference share capital amounted to CU200,000 throughout 2010 and 2011.
4. The interest payable is in respect of 12% debenture stock. The debenture holders have the right to convert their stock into ordinary shares at any time after 1 January 2013. The terms of the conversion are 20 ordinary shares of CU1.00 each for every CU50 of debenture stock.

Required:
a. Define earnings per share in accordance with the standard accounting practice.
b. Explain what is meant by bonus issue of shares and indicate its likely effect on the market price of the shares.

c. Compute the figures for earnings per share to be disclosed in the financial statements of PAC Ltd for 2011.
d. Outline the circumstances in which the obligation to compute the fully diluted earnings per share arises.
e. Compute the figures for fully diluted earnings per share to be disclosed in the financial statements of PAC Ltd for 2011.

Answer 9:
1. Earnings per share (EPS) is the profit, in 1/100 of the CU, attributable to each equity share, based on the profit (consolidated) of the period after tax, minority interest, extraordinary items and preference dividends divided by the number of equity shares in issue and ranking for dividend.

2. A bonus issue is made on a pro-rata basis, free of charge, to existing shareholders. The nominal value of the bonus issue is transferred from the distributable reserves to share capital ranking for dividend. The effect of the capitalisation or script issue is that an equivalent amount of profits are no longer available for distribution. And because the company receives no additional funds, the anticipated future income stream will be spread over a larger number of shares. The market price of the shares might therefore be expected to fall by a factor that represents the existing number of shares as a proportion of the new share capital.

3. Earnings per Share

$$2011: (128-16)/ (60 + [60 \times 5]) \times 100 = 31.11$$
$$2010: (96-16)/ (60 + [60 \times 5]) \times 100 = 22.22$$

4. At the end of an accounting period, a company may have, in issue, securities that do not, at the present point in time, have any claim to a share of equity earnings, but may give rise to such a claim in the future. Such securities include:
• A separate class of equity shares which at present is not entitled to any dividend, but will be entitled after some future date;
• Convertible loan stock or convertible preference shares which give the holders the right at some future date to exchange their securities for ordinary shares of the company, at a predetermined conversion rate.
• Options at below market price.

In these circumstances, the future number of shares ranking for a dividend might increase and cause a fall in the earnings per share. In other words, a future increase in the number of equity shares will cause a dilution, or watering down of the equity, and it is necessary to compute the fully diluted earnings per share in order to forewarn the existing equity shareholders of the effect on their financial interest should such conversion take place.

The fully diluted earnings per share need only be disclosed if the dilution is material. Dilution amounting to 5% or more of the basic earnings per share is regarded as material for this purpose.

5. Fully Diluted Earnings per Share:

2011: $\{(128 - 16^*) + [72-24^{**}]\}/[60 + (60 \times 5)] + ([600^{***}/50] \times 20]) \times 100$
$= 26.67$
2010: $\{96 -16 + (72-24)/[60 + (60 \times 5)] + (600/50 \times 20) \times 100$
$= 21.33$

Note:
* CU16 is the dividends payable to the preference shareholders which must be deducted to derive the amount available to the equity shareholders
** CU24,000 is the element of the interest payable to the debenture holders at 12% for 4 months convertible on 30th April 2011 which is added back to reflect the possible conversion to ordinary shares by removing it from the total interest payable (i.e. 72,000/12 x 4).
*** CU600,000 is the amount of 12% debenture stock derived if 12% is equal to interest payable of CU72,000(i.e. 72,000/0.12) and convertible at CU50 for every 20 ordinary shares of CU1.00 each.

Question 10:
(a.) Discuss the nature and purpose of accounting ratios.
(b.) Identify five accounting ratios that may be used to access the solvency and financial stability of a company. Give the formulae to be used for the calculation in each case.
(c.) Identify and discuss five limitations of ratio analysis.

Answer 10:

(a) Discussion would involve the following:
• The purpose of accounting ratios is to add to the knowledge that can be obtained from an examination of the figures presented in financial statements.

- Ratios are calculated by examining the relationship between two financial statements totals where there should be some kind of causal link, such as gross profit in relation to sales.
- The significance of accounting ratios is enhanced by comparison with some independent benchmark such as results achieved during a previous accounting period, by other companies, or with predetermined standards or budgets.

(b) The following five accounting ratios may be used to assess the solvency and financial stability of a company.
- Liquidity ratio – this expresses monetary assets as a ratio of current liabilities – i.e. current assets – stocks/current liabilities: 1
- Interest cover ratio – which expresses profit before interest and tax as a ratio of interest charges – i.e. profit before interest and tax/interest payable.
- Proprietary ratio – which expresses the shareholders' investment or equity in the company as a percentage of total sources of funding in the business – i.e. shareholders' funds/total sources of finance or total assets x 100%.
- Debt to Equity ratio – which expresses the non-current liabilities or net borrowings as a ratio of equity capital, and it given as:

$$\frac{\text{Loans + Preference Share Capital}}{\text{Ordinary shares + Reserves + Minority interest}}$$

OR

$$\frac{\text{Non-current Liabilities}}{\text{Equity}}$$

- Current or Working Capital Ratio – which measures the adequacy of current assets in meeting the company's short term liabilities and it is given as:

$$\frac{\text{Current Assets}}{\text{Current Liabilities}} : 1$$

(c) Five limitations of ratio analysis:
(1) Different business entities may adapt different accounting policies and may also use different methods in accounting for certain accounting items, thereby producing different figures making comparisons inappropriate (e.g. accounting periods covered, the methods used by entities to account for tangible fixed assets, stocks, development expenditure, and leases can affect ROCE, gearing and profits.)
(2) Though there are general guidelines, for instance, that the quick ratio should not be less than 1, there is no such thing as an "ideal" ratio. A quick ratio of less than 1 may be acceptable in some businesses, but may not be very low for another.
(3) Unless ratios are calculated on a uniform basis and from a uniform data, any comparisons may be inappropriate and misleading. In comparing company ratios, care must be taken to ensure that the data is consistent.
(4) Financial statements only reflect activities which can be translated in monetary terms. They therefore do not give the complete picture of the activities of the company – and therefore ratios derived may not give the complete picture and its actual position and financial strength.
(5) Ratios cannot be used as the sole test of company viability and efficiency. Using just a few financial ratios cannot provide a reliable tool for running a company and solving business problems. And relying on a few ratios may inhibit management from taking some risks to expand and grow the business to the detriment of the long-term benefit of the company.

Question 11

The following summarised data was extracted from the published financial statements of AGIP Ltd for the year ended 31 December 2010.

	CU'000
Fixed assets	2,600
Net current assets	200
	2,800
Ordinary shares of CU1 per share	1,400
7% Preference shares of CU1 per share	400
Revenue reserves	600
Shareholders' funds	2,400

8% Debentures	400

	2,800
	====
Net profit before tax	880
Taxation	(460)

Net profit after tax	420
Dividends paid and proposed:	
Ordinary shares	(180)
7% Preference shares	(27)

Retained profit for the year	213
	=====

Price per ordinary share (2010 closing quotation) was CU2.20

Required:
Calculate for each ordinary share -
(i) Book value of net assets per share
(ii) Earnings per share (EPS)
(iii) Earnings yield
(iv) Dividend yield
(v) Price earnings ratio (P/E Ratio)

Answer 11
Note: The question requires only calculation without interpretation.

AGIP Ltd:
(i) Book value of net assets per share:

	CU'000
Fixed assets	2,600
Net current assets	200
8% Debentures	(400)
7% Preference shares	(400)

Net book value of assets for ord. Shares	2,000

Number of ordinary shares	1,400

Net book value of assets per ordinary share = CU2,000/1,400 = CU1.43

(ii) EPS: to calculate this, the earnings must first be determined.

	CU'000
Profit after tax (as given)	420
7% Preference dividend	(27)
Earnings attributable to ord. Shares	293

EPS = CU293/1,400 = CU0.28 x 100 = 28 per share

(iii) Earnings yield = EPS/Price per share x 100 = 28/220 x 100 = 12.73%

(iv) Dividend yield = Dividend per share/price per share x 100
Ord. Dividend per share = Ord. Dividend/No. of Ord. Shares x100
    = CU180/1400 x 100 = 12.86
Then, dividend yield = 12.86/220.0 x 100% = 5.85%

(v) Price Earnings Ratio = Price per share/Earnings per share
    = 220.0/28.0 times = 7.86 times
(Note: this is also the inverse of the earnings yield, i.e. 100/12.73 = 7.86)

Question 12
(i) Explain the term "gearing" in relation to the capital structure of a limited liability company.
(ii) The capital employed by two different companies was as shown below:

	Daily Express Ltd CU'000	Total News Ltd CU'000
Ordinary shares of CU1 per share	600	1,800
6% Preference shares of CU1 per share	600	-
	1,200	1,800
Retained profits	800	1,200
Shareholders' funds	2,000	3,000
9% Debentures	2,000	1,000
Capital employed	4,000	4,000

Required:
(a) Calculate the gearing ratios of each company, stating in each case whether the gearing is high or low.
(b) Calculate the maximum percentage dividend on ordinary shares which each company could declare, without utilising or adding to accumulated retained profits if profit for the year ended 31 December 2010 was as follows:

	A CU'000	B CU'000
Net profit (before debenture interest and taxation)	500	1,000

Assume corporation taxation to be 30% of Net profit.

(c) State what conclusion you could draw from your calculation in ii (b)

Answer 12

(i) Gearing: For answer, see text, 3.8.3

ii (a) Gearing can be expressed in Debt/Equity Ratio as:

$$\frac{\text{Loans + Preference Share Capital}}{\text{Ordinary shares + Reserves + Minority interest}}$$

OR

$$\frac{\text{Non-current Liabilities}}{\text{Equity}}$$

	Daily Express Ltd CU'000	Total News Ltd CU'000
6% Preference shares	600	-
9% Debentures	2,000	1,000
Total fixed debts	2,600	1,000
Ordinary shares	600	1,800
Gearing	2,600/600 = 4.33: 1 High	1,000/1,800 = 0.56: 1 Low

ii (b) Maximum percentage Dividend payable on ordinary shares

	Daily Express Ltd CU'000		Total News Ltd CU'000	
	A	B	A	B
Net profit before debenture interest and Tax	500	1,000	500	1,000
Less: 9% Debenture interest	(180)	(180)	(90)	(90)
Net profit before taxation	320	820	410	910
Less: Corporation tax at 30%	(96)	(246)	(123)	(273)
Net profit after tax	224	574	287	637
Less: 6% Preference share dividend	(36)	(36)	-	-
Earnings available for ordinary shareholders	188	538	287	637
Percentage dividend	$\frac{188}{600}$ %	$\frac{538}{600}$ %	$\frac{287}{1,800}$ %	$\frac{637}{1,800}$ %
	31.33%	89.67%	15.94%	35.39%

	A	B	A	B
EPS:	188/600 x 100 = 31.33	538/600x100 = 89.67	287/1800x100 = 15.94	637/1800x100 = 35.39

(c) Conclusions

It can be seen that in the Daily Express Ltd, the highly geared company, the EPS is significantly better than in the Total News Ltd which has a low gearing, though both companies have the same level of net profit before interest and corporate tax charges. When the net profit before interest and tax doubled, Total News Ltd's EPS increased approximately 2.2 times while that of Daily Express Ltd rose almost three times (by 2.87 times). This illustrates the fact that in a highly geared company like the Daily Express Ltd, EPS responds disproportionately to the increase or decrease in the net profit before interest and tax.

Question 13

Detroit is a manufacturing company. Its latest balance sheet and profit and loss account summary is as follows:

Detroit Ltd
Balance Sheet as at 31 March 2010

	CU'000		CU'000
Authorised Capital:		Fixed Assets -	
800,000 CU1 Ordinary shares	800	Freehold property	
	===	(book value)	480
Issued and fully paid		Plant and machinery	
400,000 CU1 Ord. Shares	400	(cost less depr)	800
Capitral Reserves	200	Motor vehicles	
Revenue Reserves	800	(cost less depr.)	200
		Office furniture	
		(cost less depr.)	200
Shareholders' funds	1,400	Current Assets CU'000	
Loan Capital:		Stocks 1,000	
400,000 10% Debentures		Debtors 400	
(secured on the freehold property 400		Investments 120	1,520
And repayable in 2022)			
Book value of long term funds	1,800		
Current liabilities: CU'000			
Trade creditors 238.4			
Bank overdraft 878.4			
Current taxation 176.0			
Dividend payable 107.2	1,400		
	3,200		3,200
	=====		=====

Summary Profit and Loss Account for the year ended 31 March 2010

	CU'000
Sales (all on credit)	4,000
Profit after charging all expenses except debenture interest	440
Less: Debenture interest	40
Profit before taxation	400

Less: Corporation tax on the taxable profit for the year	176

Profit after taxation	224
Less: Ordinary dividend proposed	107.2

Retained profits transferred to revenue reserve	116.8
	======

Notes:
1. Purchases for the year were CU2,160,000.
2. Cost of sales for the year was 3,000,000.
3. The market price of a Detroit Ltd ordinary share at 31 March 2010 was CU4.00.
4. Income tax is to be taken at 33%. Advance corporation tax to be ignored.
5. The company estimates the current value of its Freehold property at CU880,000.
6. The Managing Director has suggested that a figure representing the company's goodwill be computed and included in the balance sheet under that heading with the Shareholders' funds increased by its value.

Required:

a. Compute the following ratios:
(i) Primary ratio (using the book value of total assets as capital employed).
(ii) Secondary ratio – the profit margin
(iii) Secondary ratio – the turnover of capital.
(iv) Current ratio.
(v) Liquid ratio.
(vi) Debtors ratio.
(vii) Proprietary ratio.
(viii) Stock turnover ratio.
(ix) Dividend yield.
(x) Price Earnings ratio and its reciprocal.

b. Write a brief comment on the liquidity of Detroit Ltd, stating the reference points to which relevant ratios can be compared.

Answer 13

a. (i) Primary ratio =
Net operating profit/Capital employed (Total Assets) x 100%
= 440,000/3,200,000 x 100% = 13.75%

(ii) Secondary ratio (Profit margin) = Net operating profit/Sales x 100%
= 440,000/4,000,000 x100% = 11.00%

(iii) Secondary ratio (Turnover of capital) = Sales/Capital employed (Total Assets)
= 4,000,000/3,200,000 = 1.25 times

(iv) Current ratio = Current assets/Current liabilities: 1
= 1,520,000/1,400,000 = 1.08:1

(v) Liquid ratio = Current assets – stock/Current liabilities: 1
= 1,520,000 – 1,000,000/1,400,000 : 1 = 0.37 : 1

(vi) Debtors ratio = Credit sales/Debtors
= 4,000,000/400,000 = 10 times = 365/10 = 36.5 days

(vii) Proprietary ratio = Shareholders funds/Total assets
= 1,400,000/3,200,000 = 0.44

(viii) Stock turnover ratio = Cost of sales/Average stock

Average stock: Purchases	CU 2,160,000
Less: Cost of sales	3,000,000
Stock decrease during the year	(840,000)
Therefore, Closing stock =	1,000,000
Plus half the decrease (1/2 x 840,000)	420,000
Average stock	1,420,000

Stock turnover = 3,000,000/1,420,000 = 2.11 times

(ix) Dividend yield = Dividend/Market value of shares
= CU107,200/(400,000 x CU4.00) x 100% = 6.70%

(x) Price Earnings ratio = Market value of shares/Earnings
= (400,000 x CU4.00)/224,000 = 7.14

(Note, this has been worked out on the basis of the total figures as they were more readily available instead of on the more usual basis of per share figures.)

The reciprocal of price earnings ratio is known as the earnings yield and it is equal to:
Earnings/Market value of shares x 100%
CU224,000/(400,000 x CU4.00) x 100% = 14.00%

b. Brief comment on the liquidity of Detroit Ltd.

The liquidity of the company depends on the terms of the overdraft facility. If the facility is dischargeable at short notice, the company will have a highly illiquid condition at 0.37: 1. But if it has been granted an extended term for the overdraft, the liquidity position improves nominally to 1:1 (1,520,000 – 1,000,000/(1,400,000 – 878,400) : 1 = 520,000/521,600 :1

When the timing of the cash inflows and out flows is considered, the liquidity position of the company improves slightly further. If the creditors allow the company an average of 40 days for settlement (CU238,400/CU2,160,000 x 365 days), they are adequately matched by the debtors taking of just over 36 days to settle.

The dividend is payable only after the Annual General Meeting – this means time saving of at least six months, and the corporation tax is not due for at least another nine months.

The company's ratios could be compared with the actuals calculated for the previous periods, with the forecasts or budgeted figures and with those of similar companies in the same industry or the industry average.

Question 14

The summarised financial statements of two retailing companies in the same industry for the year ended 31 December 2010 are as overleaf:

Trading, Profit and Loss Accounts for the year ended 31 December 2010

	Company X		Company Y	
	CU'000	CU'000	CU'000	CU'000
Sales		400,000		400,000
Opening stock	64,000		16,000	
Purchases	312,000		300,000	
	376,000		316,000	
Less: Closing Stock	96,000		24,000	
Cost of sales		280,000		292,000
Gross Profit		120,000		108,000
Less: Expenses		94,800		84,960
Net profit		25,200		23,040

Balance Sheet as at 31 December 2010

	Company X		Company Y	
	CU'000	CU'000	CU'000	CU'000
Fixed assets (written down values)		260,000		160,000
Current assets:				
Stocks	96,000		24,000	
Debtors	34,000		8,500	
Bank	10,000		39,500	
	140,000		72,000	
Less: Current liabilities	40,000	100,000	40,000	32,000
		360,000		192,000
Share Capital		160,000		160,000
Reserves		200,000		32,000
		360,000		192,000

Required:

a. Fill out the appropriate figures, with workings, in the table shown below:

	Company X	Company Y
Current ratio		
Liquidity ratio		
Rate of Stock turnover		
Gross Profit to Turnover %		
Net Profit to Turnover %		
Net Profit to Capital Employed %		

b. One of the companies is a Costcutter Store which has adopted the policy of selling goods as cheaply as possible in order to increase the turnover. The other company is a Premium Store which occupies a high class site, gives special attention to customer service and charges high end prices for its goods.

Required:

State, with reasons, which of these companies is Company X and which is Company Y in question (a) above.

Answer 14.

(a)

	Company X	Company Y
Current ratio	= 140,000/40,000 : 1 = 3.5 : 1	72,000/40,000 : 1 = 1.8 : 1
Liquidity ratio	= 44,000/40,000 : 1 = 1.1 : 1	48,000/40,000 : 1 = 1.2 : 1
Rate of Stock Turnover	= 280,000/1/2(64,000 + 96,000) = 3.5 times	292,000/1/2(16,000 + 24,000) = 14.6 times
Gross Profit %	= 120,000/400,000 x 100% = 30%	108,000/400,000 x 100% = 27%
Net Profit %	= 25,200/400,000 x 100% = 6.30%	23,040/400,000 x 100% = 5.76%
Net Profit to Capital employed %	= 25,200/360,000 x 100% = 7.00%	23,040/192,000 x 100% = 12.00%

(b)

	Premium Store: Company Y	Costcutter Store: Company X
1	Stocks and sells a wider range of expensive items. As a result, stock turnover is slower.	The company's lower prices encourage sales which do not need the support of high stock level. The faster stock turnover is the result of the company being in business with only a quarter of the stock level of its rival.
2	There is an increased investment in fixed assets, resulting from ownership of premium site and prestigious premises. This accounted for the relatively low return on capital employed.	

Question 15

The financial details provided below are for two companies operating in similar retail business. They use similar business and accounting policies.

Balance Sheets as at 30 June 2010

	Betterware Ltd CU'000	Homeware Ltd CU'000
Share Capital and Reserves:		
Issued shares	700	940
Capital reserves	130	70
Revenue reserves	370	574
10% Debentures	310	128
Current Liabilities:		
Bank overdraft	42	40
Trade Creditors	194	264
Other Current liabilities and Provisions	84	96
	1,630	2,112

Fixed assets at book values:			
Land and Buildings	572		762
Plant and Equipment	436		684
Motor Vehicles	118		124
Current Assets:			
Stock	244		194
Trade Debtors	248		332
Cash	12		16
	1,630		2,112

Profit and Loss Accounts for the year ended 30 June 2010

	Betterware Ltd		Homeware ltd	
	CU'000	CU'000	CU'000	CU'000
Sales		1,494		1,140
Opening stock	204		184	
Purchases	1,176		762	
	1,380		946	
Less: Closing stock	244		192	
		1,136		754
Gross Profit		358		386
Operating Expenses:				
Selling and distribution	128		120	
Admin and Mgt	62		58	
Financial	18	208	16	194
Net Profit		150		192
Provision for taxation		74		90
Net profit after tax		76		102
Provision for dividend		48		74
Transfer to Revenue Reserve		28		28

Required:
(i) Calculate for each company six ratios which you consider most appropriate for indicating the efficiency of operations and short-term financial strength of the two companies, showing the figures you have used and pointing out any weakness in the figures, and alternatives that might be taken had more information been available.

(ii) Using the financial information provided above and the ratios you have calculated, prepare a report which analyses and compares the efficiency of operations and short term financial strength of Betterware Ltd and Homeware Ltd.

Answer 15
(Note: This question requires you to use ratio analysis to compare the performance and liquidity of two separate companies. Question (i) specifically requires just six ratios to be calculated out of the so many that can be calculated. Different analysts would choose different ratios, but the main issue is that there should be a reasonable selection.

(i)   **Betterware Ltd**   **Homeware Ltd**
Efficiency Ratios:
A. Gross Profit %:
Gross Profit/Sales x 100% = 358/1,494 x 100% = 23.96%
                          = 386/1,140 x 100%   = 33.85%

B. Net Profit before Tax %:
NPBT/Net Capital Employed = 150/1,310 x 100% = 11.45%
                          = 192/1,712 x 100% = 11.21%
(NCE = Shareholders Fund + Debentures
Or Fixed Assets + Current assets minus
Current liabilities)

C. Net Asset Turnover:
Sales/Net Capital Employed   = 1,494/1,310: 1 = 1.14: 1
                              = 1,140/1,712: 1 = 0.66: 1

Short-term financial strength ratios:

D. Liquidity ratio:
Current assets − stock/Current liabilities
                          = 260/320: 1 = 0.81: 1
                                            = 348/400: 1 = 0.87: 1

                            Betterware Ltd   Homeware Ltd
E. Debtors' turnover ratio =
Trade debtors/Credit sales x 365 days
            = 248/1,494 x 365 days = 60.6 days
                        = 32/1,140 x 365 days = 106.30 days

F. Creditors' turnover ratio =
Trade creditors/Credit purchases x 365 days
            = 194/1,176 x 365 days = 60.2 days
                        = 264/762 x 365 days= 126.46 says

The major weakness in these figures is the ratios were calculated on the basis of historical data prepared under the historical cost convention. As a result of this, one company is much older than the other and this age differential, other things being equal, would have impact in making it have better efficiency ratios based on the fact that its total assets and capital employed will be less than those of the other company since a higher level of depreciation would have been accumulated over the years.

If more information were available, figures based on current cost account could have been used, and this could have taken inflation into account and would have made the figures from both companies time comparable.

(ii) **Report on the efficiency of operation and short-term financial strength of the companies:**

Efficiency of operations
In real terms, Homeware Ltd achieved a better net profit figure (CU192,000) on a lower turnover of CU1,140,000. Betterware ltd achieved CU150,000 on a turnover of CU1,494,000. This represents a net profit percentage of 16.85% and 10.00% for Homeware and Betterware Ltd respectively. The main contributor to this situation is the high gross profit percentage: 23.96% for Betterware Ltd, and 33.85% for Homeware ltd. As both companies are in the same business, this in variation in the GP% is very significant. It could well be that Betterware Ltd might be underpricing its goods, while Homeware Ltd is overpricing theirs. And it is possible that both companies could improve their profitability by adjusting their prices.

Betterware Ltd's lower GP% appears to be the cause for the very fast stock turnover of 5.07 times: (1,136,000 ÷1/2(204,000+244,000); Homeware Ltd's

Stock turnover was 4.0times: (754,000 ÷ 1/2(184,000+192,000). Homeware Ltd's lower turnover and slower stock turnover are reflected in its poor sales to net capital employed ratio of 0.66 compared with Betterware Ltd's 1.14 times.

Short-term Financial strength
The liquidity ratios show that both companies are weak (Betterware Ltd: 0.81:1; Homeware Ltd: 0.87:1). Even when the overdraft is set aside, improvement in the ratios will still be marginal.

The debtors' collection period and creditors' settlement days are balanced out for Betterware Ltd (about 60 days for each). Those for Homeware Ltd are 106 days and 126 days respectively. This is too high. As both companies are in comparable business, there might be the need for Homeware Ltd to reconsider its strategy and reduce this period, at least by 50%.
To remedy the apparent liquidity problem, both companies might consider the issuance of additional share capital, or debentures (if they have the collateral security to back up any long term loans.

Question 16
Total Merchandising Company Ltd has recently reorganised the management team, due mainly to the low profitability in the recent years. As an analyst, you have been asked to analyse the company's financial position and the most recent financial statements are produced below, together with the average ratios for the industry.

Industry Average Ratios
Current ratio	2:1
Quick ratio	1:1
Debt to total assets	30%
Times interest earned	7 times
Fixed charges coverage	5 times
Stock turnover	10 times
Average collection period	15 days
Fixed assets turnover	6 times
Total assets turnover	3 times
Net profit on sales	3%
Return on total assets	9%
Return on net worth	12.8%

Total Merchandising Company Ltd
Income Statement for the year ended 31 December 2010

	CU'000	CU'000
Sales		15,900
Less: Cost of Sales		13,200
Gross Profit		2,700
Operating expenses	1,470	
Depreciation	240	
Interest	90	1,800
Net Profit before taxation		900
Taxation		450
Undistributed profits after tax		450

Balance Sheet as at 31 December 2010

	CU'000	CU'000	CU'000
Fixed Assets:			
Plant and Equipment			4,500
Less: Depreciation			1,560
			2,940
Current Assets:			
Stock	3,180		
Debtors	1,320		
Marketable securities	660		
Cash	900	6,060	
Less: Current Liabilities:			
Sundry liabilities	420		
Creditors	900		
Notes payable (6%)	900	2,220	3,840
			6,780

Represented by:
Ordinary Share Capital   2,280
Undistributed profits   4,020

                                                                    6,300
5% Debentures   480

                                                                    6,780
                                                                  =======

Required:
A. Calculate the ratios which you feel would be useful in your analysis
B. Examine the income statement and balance sheet with a view to ascertaining the reasons for the low profits
C. State with reasons which specific ratios seem to be most out of line in their relationships to other companies in the industry.

Answer 16
Note: This thrust of this question is to use ratio analysis to compare the performance of a specified company with the industry average.

A. **Useful Ratios selected**

	Total Merchandising Company Ltd	Industry Average (given)
1. Current Ratio - 6,060/2,220: 1	2.73: 1	2: 1
2. Quick Ratio - 2,880/2,220: 1	1.3: 1	1: 1
3. Debt to Total Asset Ratio%:		
= 2,220 + 480/2,940 + 6,060		
= 2,700/9,000 x 100%	30.0%	30.0%
4. Times Interest earned:		
= 900+90/90 times	11 times	7 times
5. Fixed charge coverage –		
= 900+90+240/90+240 times	3.73 times	5 times
6. Stock turnover ratio –		
= 13,200/3,180 times	4.15 times	10 times
7. Average collection period –		
= 1,320/15,900 x 365 days	30.30 days	15 days
8. Fixed Assets turnover –		
= 15,900/2,940 times	5.41 times	6 times
9. Total Assets turnover –		
= 15,900/(2,949+6,060) times	1.76 times	3 times

10. Net Profit on Sales – = 900/15,900 x 100%	5.66%	3.0%
11. Return on Total Assets – 900/(2,940+6,060) x 100%	10%	9.0%
12. Return on Net Worth - = 900/6,780 x 100%	13.27%	12.8%

Ratios 1 – 5 above give signs of the company's good financial position. The long term position of the company also seems stable. Only 30% of its funding is provided by external investors. Both the current and quick ratios indicate a strong position in the short run, and the interest payment is sufficiently covered by the profits.

B. The combination of the low gross margin (16.98% i.e. 2,700/15,900 x 100%) and the low stock turnover (4.15 times) accounted for the low profit figure. Other companies in the industry are able to manage their stock levels at about 50% lower than Total Merchandising Company Ltd to achieve the same level of profit. Reducing the stock level and debtors balance together with a possible liquidation of the marketable securities would release more funds into the business which could be used for more profitable activities, especially in the paying off of the debentures and saving pay out by way of interest. If these measures are adopted, there is the possibility of improved stock turnover, fixed assets turnover, total assets turnover and the overall profitability of the company.

C. From the above calculations, the ratios most out of line with the industry average are: the stock turnover ratio; average collection period; and total assets turnover ratio.

Question 17
The summarised balance sheet of Conway Ltd, together with extracts from their profit and loss account for the year ended 30 June 2010 are as stated below. The two young directors of the company have made loans to the company to the full extent of their personal resources and currently require funding for a large contract worth CU120,000 from a reputable customer.
They have applied to their bank for an unsecured overdraft limit of CU30,000 to finance the contract. They have offered the bank manager their personal guarantees and the postponement of their own loans. They do not wish to offer a secured debenture as they feel this would precipitate action from the company creditors.

You are employed by the bank in its local branch office as the accountant advisor to the bank manager in the branch, in respect of requests of this nature.

You are required to write a report to the bank manager:
a. Analysing the information available to you, in the context of the request made; and
b. Advising him of the risk to the bank in granting the overdraft.

Conway Ltd
Balance Sheet as at 31 December 2010

	CU'000	CU'000
Share Capital – Ordinary shares of CU1 fully paid		6,000
Profit and loss account		1,000
		7,000
Loans by Directors		11,000
Current Liabilities:		
Accrued Expenses	10,000	
Trade Creditors	110,000	
		120,000
		138,000
Fixed Assets:		
Plant and Machinery (cost less depreciation)	21,000	
Motor Vehicles (cost less depreciation)	3,000	
Goodwill	3,600	
		27,600
Current Assets:		
Cash at Bank	23,600	
Trade Debtors	34,000	
Stocks and work in progress	47,000	
Prepayments	4,000	
Preliminary expenses	1,800	110,000
		138,000

Extracts from the Profit and Loss Account for the year ended 30 June 2010:

Sales CU460,000; Purchases of stock 280,000
Profit for the year –
after all expenses including
the ones stated below   CU9,100
Provision for corporation tax   –
Provision for depreciation of assets   3,600
Provision for directors' remuneration 12,800

Answer 17
(a)

INTERNAL REPORT

To: Manager
From: Danny Jack (Accountant)
Date: xx – xx – 20xx

Subject: Re: Conway Ltd – Application for an Overdraft Facility

This report and the conclusion reached are based on the financial ratios derived from the analysis of the financial data of Conway Ltd as provided for the period ended 31 December 2010.

The bank would want to be assured that the company is financially sound in the long-term; that the company's liquidity position in the short-term is strong; and that the company is profitable. The overriding consideration in this case is the degree of risk involved in granting the overdraft facility.

Long-term
The external liability of CU131,000, made up of current liabilities (CU120,000) and directors' loans (CU11,000), exceeds the total tangible assets of CU128,600 (total assets less goodwill, prepayments, and preliminary expenses); the liabilities are also 18.7 times greater than the shareholders' funds. (131,000/7000: 1 = 18.71: 1) The Shareholders' funds financed only 5.4% of those assets.
(7,000/128,600 times = 0.054 times (i.e. 5.4%)).

On the long-term basis, the company therefore is unsustainable and dangerously close to insolvency and possible liquidation.

Short-term Liquidity

Assuming that all sales were made on credit terms, the trade debtors were collectable within 27 days. (34,000/460,000 x 365 days = 27 days – just under a one-month period)

But assuming all the purchases were are also made on credit terms, the settlement of creditors' averages between 143 and 144 days – over a four-month period - (110,000/280,000 x 365 days = 143 days).

Even when the debtors paid off their debts timely, the company seems to be having severe difficulty paying their own trade creditors.

These conditions, together with the negative working capital and insufficient bank balance amply suggest that the company is nearing the point of liquidation.

Other Issues

At a glance, the profitability of the company appears to be good – a little above 50%.
(Net profit before tax/Net Capital Employed x 100%, i.e. 9,100/18,000 x 100% = 50.56 %.)

But this position has been produced by a major reliance on externally borrowed funds. If the profitability is calculated on the basis of the total tangible assets, a new situation arises, namely 7.08%. (Net profit before tax/Tangible Assets x 100%, i.e. 9,100/128,600 x 100% = 7.08%).

This is not encouraging enough.

b. Conclusion and advice

Based on the above facts, the business can hardly be considered a going concern, one of the four fundamental accounting concepts. The degree of risk of loss to the bank is very high. Therefore, the application for overdraft facility should be rejected.

Signed: (Danny Jack)

Part 5
CASH FLOW STATEMENTS

5.1 Purpose of Cash Flow Statements

Users of financial statements seek information about investing, financing and operating activities that a company has undertaken during the reporting period. This information helps in assessing how well the company is able to generate cash and cash equivalents and how it uses those cash flows. The cash flow statement provides this kind of information.

International Financial Reporting Standard Issue One (FRS 1) requires that "large" reporting entities to include a cash flow statement in their financial statements. The objective is to ensure that reporting entities:
• Report their cash generation and cash absorption for a period by highlighting the significant components of cash flow in a way that facilitates comparison of the cash flow performance of different businesses.
• Provide information that assists in assessment of their liquidity, solvency and financial adaptability.

The cash flow statement reports all movements in cash during the reporting period and reflects changes in both the income statement and balance sheet. In an instance, Cash Flow equals: Net Income **minus** Increase in Working Capital **minus** Investment in Fixed Assets **plus** Increase in Debts **plus** Increase in Equity.

Cash flow Summary Table

Changes In →	Income Statement		Balance Sheet			
	Operations		Investments	Financing		
Sources Of Cash	Net Income	Decrease in Working Capital	Sale of Fixed Assets	Increase in Debts	Increase in Equity	C A S H
Uses Of Cash	Losses	Increase in Working Capital	Investments in Fixed Assets	Decrease in Debts – Paying Back creditors	Decrease in Equity – Buying back	F L O W

It is possible for a company to report a negative cash flow despite a positive net profit. There may be a variety of reasons for such a finding including, among others:
- Acquisitions;
- High capital expenditure in the case of rapidly expanding operations; and
- Repayment of a large amount of maturing debts.

However, it is important to consider the cash flow trends of the company under analysis. Ultimately, returns to investors, liquidity and solvency are functions of cash flows and a company leaking cash can lose confidence amongst the investors, analysts, and even the customers. There are also cases of companies that present a net profit becoming insolvent due to cash flow difficulties.

To help achieve the objective of cash flow reporting, FRS 1 requires that individual cash flows are classified under certain standard headings according to the activity that gave rise to them. The standard headings required in a cash flow statement (also shown under three broad headings of Operating, Investing and Financing activities) are:

- Operating activities.
- Dividends from joint ventures and associates – relevant only for the cash flow statements of groups.
- Returns on investments and servicing of finance.
- Taxation.
- Capital expenditure and financial investment.
- Acquisitions and disposals.
- Equity dividends paid.
- Management of liquid resources.
- Financing.

Showing the cash flows under these standard headings ensures that cash flows are reported in a form that highlights their major components and facilitates comparison of the cash flow performance of different businesses.

Cash flows relating to the management of liquid resources and financing can be combined under a single heading, provided that the cash flows relating to each are shown separately and separate subtotals are given.

Each cash flow should be classified according to the substance of the transaction giving rise to it.

The substance of a transaction determines the most appropriate standard heading under which to report cash flows that are not specific in the standard categories.

It is important to have clear definition of cash in relation to cash flow statements.

Cash means cash in hand and deposits repayable on demand with any qualifying financial institutions, less overdrafts from any qualifying institutions repayable on demand. Deposits are repayable on demand if they can be withdrawn at any time without notice and without penalty, or if the maturity or period of notice of not more than 24 hours or one working day has been agreed upon. Cash includes cash in hand and deposits denominated in foreign currencies.

An overdraft is a borrowing facility repayable on demand that is used by drawing on a current account with a qualifying financial institution.

A qualifying institution is an entity that as part of its business receives deposits or other repayable funds and grants credits for its own account.

Cash flow is an increase or decrease in the amount of cash.
The practical effect of these definitions is that the cash flow statement carries only the inflows and outflows of "pure" cash items. Short-term deposits and loans are not included within the definition of cash.

Included in the FRS1 is this illustration which shows a cash flow statement for a single company, and illustrates the standard headings and examples of items within the standard headings.

5.2 The illustration includes the reconciliations and notes required by the FRS 1. Note 1 gives the components of the net cash flows reported under each heading. These can be shown on the face of the cash flow statement or in the notes.

XYZ Ltd
Cash Flow Statement for the Year ended 31 December 20x11

Reconciliation of operating profit to net cash inflow from operating activities

	CU 000
Operating profit	6,022
Depreciation Charges	899

Increase in Stock	(194)
Increase in Debtors	(72)
Increase in Creditors	234
Net cash inflow from operation Activities	6,889

Cash Flow Statement

Net cash inflow from operating activities	6,889
Returns on investments and servicing of finance (note 1)	2,999
Taxation	(2,922)
Capital Expenditure (note 1)	(1,525)
	5,441
Equity Dividends paid	(2,417)
	3,024
Management of liquid resources (note 1)	(450)
Financing (Note 1)	57
Increase in Cash	2,631

Reconciliation of net cash flow to movement in net debt (note 2)

Increase in cash in the period	2,631
Cash to repurchase debenture	149
Cash used to increase liquid resources	450
Change in net debt	3,230
Net debt at 1 January 20X11	(2,903)
Net funds at 31 December 20X12	327

Notes to Cash Flow Statements
(1) Gross cash flows

	CU000	CU 000
Returns on investments and servicing of finance		
Interest received	3,011	
Interest paid	(12)	2,999
Capital Expenditure		
Payments to acquire intangible fixed assets	(71)	
Payments to acquire tangible fixed assets	(1,496)	
Receipts from sales of tangible fixed assets	42	(1,525)
Management of liquid resources		
Purchase of treasury bills	(650)	
Sale of treasury bills	200	(450)
Financing		
Issue of ordinary share capital		211
Repurchase of debenture loan		(149)
Expenses paid in connection with share issues		(5)
		57

(2) Analysis of changes in net debt

	At 1 Jan. 20X12 CU 000	Cash flows CU 000	Other changes CU 000	At 31 Dec. 20X12 CU 000
Cash in hand and at Bank	42	847	-	889
Overdrafts	(1,784)	1,784		
		2,631		
Debts due within a year	(149)	149	(230)	(230)
Due after one year	(1,262)		230	(1,032)
Current asset investment	250	450		700
Total	(2,903)	(3,230)	-	327

5.3 Components of the Cash Flows

5.3.1 Operating Activities

Cash flows from operating activities are generally the cash effects of transactions and other events relating to the operating or trading activities. Net cash flow from operating activities represents the net increase or decrease in cash resulting from the operations shown in the profit and loss account in arriving at the operating profit. The operating cash flows may be reported in cash flow statement on a net or gross basis.

Reconciliation between the operating profit, which for non-financial companies is normally the profit before interest, reported in the profit and loss account and the net cash flow from operating activities should be given. This should disclose separately the movements in stocks, debtors and creditors as relate to operating activities.

In reporting net cash flows from operating activities, two possible methods can be applied. These are: the direct (Gross) method; and the indirect (Net) method.

The direct method shows the actual receipts and payments, including cash receipts from customers, cash payments to suppliers and cash payments to and on behalf of employees, which make up the net cash flow from operating activities. The indirect method starts with operating profit and adjusted for non-cash charges and credits to reconcile to the net cash flow from operating activities.

The two methods produce the same result; the only difference is as regards the derivation of the item, Net Cash Inflow from Operating Activities.

Comparison is as follows:

Direct Method	CU	Indirect Method	CU
Cash received from customers	15,424	Operating profit	6,022
Cash payments to suppliers	(5,824)	Depreciation charges	899
Cash paid to and on behalf of employees	(2,200)	Increase in stocks	(194)
		Increase in debtors	(72)
Other cash payments	(511)	Increase in creditors	234
Net cash inflow from Operating activities	6,889		6,889

The direct method has the advantage of showing the operating cash receipts and payments. The knowledge of the specific sources of cash receipts and the purpose for which the cash payments were made in the past period may be useful in assessing future cash flows. These information are not shown anywhere else in the financial statements. Besides, the method indeed show the true cash flows involved in the trading operations of the reporting entity.

The only disadvantage of this method is that there may be a material cost in preparing the information, as it is not revealed elsewhere in the financial statements.

The indirect method, on the other hand, has the advantage of highlighting the differences between operating profit and net cash flow from operating activities. Used in combination with the notes reconciling the operating profit to the net cash flow from operating activities, the user can easily relate trading profits to the cash flow and thus understand the quality of the earnings made by the reporting entity during the period. Reconciliation is important in order to give an indication of the quality of the company's earnings. Besides, some investors and creditors assess future cash flows by estimating future income and then allowing for the adjustment accruals. So, the information obtained from the past accruals adjustments may become handy in estimating future adjustments. Additionally, there is a low cost in preparing the information. The only disadvantage of the method is that it lacks information on the significant elements of the trading cash flows.

The IFRS therefore requires that the cash flow statement shows the net cash flow from operating activities and accompanied with a reconciliation of operating profit for the period to the net cash flow from operating activities.

To calculate the operating profit, the accrual concept is used. Net cash flow from operating activities only bears the cash inflows and out flows arising from trading. Net cash inflow can be derived from either:
• The accounting records of the reporting entity by adding up the cash receipts and payments directly, or
• Operating profit can be adjusted by the relevant amounts in the profit and loss account and the opening and closing balance sheets which represent the differences between cash flows and amount accrued.

In most cases, the latter approach is quicker and easier; and also gives rise to the reconciliation statement which is required by the IFRS.

The following are the main categories of items in the profit and loss account and on the balance sheet which form part of the reconciliation between operating profit and net cash flow from operating activities.

1. Depreciation – This is the book value written off of capital expenditure. While capital expenditure is recorded under "Capital Expenditure" at the time of the cash out flow, depreciation represents an addition to the operating profit in arriving at the cash inflow.
2. Profit/Loss on disposal of fixed assets – The cash inflow from a sale is recorded under capital expenditure. In line with the provision of the IFRS 3, most profits and losses on disposal are no longer included in the operating profit; sometimes it may be necessary to adjust operating profit. A loss on disposal is added to operating profit; a profit on disposal is deducted from operating profit.
3. Change in the balance sheet debtors – When a sale is made, irrespective of the date cash is received, an income is created. If the cash is not received by the balance sheet date, there is no cash inflow from operating activities for the current accounting period. In the same way, the opening debtors represent sales of previous accounting period, most of which will be cash receipts in the current period. The change between opening and closing debtors will represent the adjustment required to move from the operating profit to net cash inflow.

An increase in debtors is a deducted from operating profit. This is because more sales are not being received in cash in the current period than are being brought forward from the previous period. **A decrease in debtors** is an addition to operating profit.

4. Change in the balance sheet stocks – Stock at the balance sheet date represents a purchase which has not actually been charged against current operating profits. Since cash was spent on the purchase or a creditor incurred, it does represent an actual or potential cash outflow. An increase in stocks is a deduction from operating profit in the same way as an increase in debtors; a decrease in stocks is an addition to operating profit (as an increase in trade creditors).
5. Change in balance sheet trade creditors – A purchase represents the incurring of expenditure and a charge or potential charge to the profit and loss account. It does not represent a cash outflow until paid. To the extent that purchase results in a charge to the profit and loss account, an increase in creditors between the two balance sheet dates is an addition to the operating profit, while a decrease is a deduction.

Note that the fixed assets creditors are not included in the reconciliation of operating profit to net cash inflow as they not result in a charge to the profit and loss of the current period.

5.3.2 Example
Q. BYZ is a new company. It made an operating profit of CU600,000 in its first year. Extracts from the closing balance sheet are as shown below.
Required: Determine the net cash inflow from its operating activities.

Debtors	CU250,000
Stock	236,000
Creditors	270,000

An analysis of creditors showed:

For raw materials	CU205,400
For fixed assets	24,000
For various expenses	27,000
Accruals	13,600
	270,000

Answer:
BYZ Cash inflow from operating activities

Operating Profit	CU 600,000
Increase in stocks	(236,000)
Increase in debtors	(250,000)
Increase in creditors (270,000 – 24,000)	246,000
Net cash inflow from operating activities	CU360,000

5.3.3 Reporting entities may use the direct method for reporting net cash flow from operating activities. In that case, they must in addition disclose the reconciliation required by the indirect method. The relevant cash flow here can be derived from: the accounting records of the entity by totalling the cash receipts and payments directly; or by the opening and closing balance sheets and profit and loss account for the year by building up the summary control accounts for: Sales (to determine cash received from customers); Purchases (to determine cash payments to suppliers); and Wages (to determine cash paid to and on behalf of employees).

5.3.4 Example: The balance sheets of RTB Ltd are as follows:

	Year 1 CU	Year 2 CU
Fixed Assets	306,728	298,728
Stocks	-	-
Debtors	531,680	692,000
Cash	-	330,332
Creditors	(438,408)	(637,780)
	400,0000	683,280
Share Capital	400,000	400,000
Reserves	-	283,280
	400,000	683,280

Extracts from the profit and loss account for the year are as follows:

	CU	CU
Sales		3,178,894
Cost of sales:		
Purchases (no stocks)	2,043,660	
Wages and salaries	291,800	
Depreciation	168,000	
		(2,503,460)
Administration expenses:		
Purchases	192,154	
Salaries	200,000	
		(392,154)
Operating profit and retained profit for the year		283,280

Notes:

	Year 1	year 2
1. Creditors:		
Creditors from purchases ledger:		
Fixed Assets	-	92,000
Others	421,128	516,480
PAYE creditor	17,280	29,300

2. Purchase invoices relating to fixed assets totalling CU160,000 have been posted to the purchases ledger during the year.

Required:
Prepare the cash flow statement using the direct method and a note reconciling operating profit to the net cash inflow from operating activities.

Answer: **RTB Ltd – Cash Flow Statement (Direct Method)**

Operating activities
Cash received from customers (see Working 1)	CU3,018,574
Cash payment to suppliers (see Working 2)	(2,140,462)
Cash paid to and on behalf of employees (see Working 3)	(479,780)
Net cash inflow from operating activities	398,332

Capital Expenditure:
Purchase of fixed assets (see Working 4)	(68,000)
	330,332

Reconciliation of Operating Profit to Net Cash Inflow from Operating Activities

Operating Profit	CU 283,280
Depreciation charges	168,000
Increase in stock	-
Increase in Debtors	(160,320)
Increase in Creditors	107,372
Net Cash Inflow from Operating Activities	398,332

Workings:

Working 1

Sales Ledger Control

	CU		CU
Debtors balance b/d	531,680	Cash Receipt	3,018,574
Sales	3,178,894	Balance c/d	692,000
	3,710,574		3,710,574
	========		========

Working 2

Purchases Ledger Control (excluding fixed asset purchases)

	CU		CU
Cash paid (bal fig)	2,140,462	Creditors balance b/d	421,128
Balance c/d (creditors)	516,480	Purchases:	
		Cost of sales	2,043,660
		Administration	192,154
	2,656,942		2,656,942
	========		=========

Working 3

Wages Control

	CU		CU
Net Wages and PAYE paid		Balance b/d (PAYE)	17,280
(bal figure)	479,780	Cost of Sales	291,800
Balance c/d (PAYE)	29,300	Administration	200,000
	509,080		509,080
	======		======

Working 4

Fixed Assets Expenditure:
Cash paid for fixed assets is a total of:

CU160,000 – 92,000 = CU68,000.

The CU160,000 invoice agrees with the movement in fixed assets per the balance sheets.

Fixed Assets – Net Book Value

	CU		CU
Balance b/d	306,728	Depreciation charge	168,000
Additional purchases (Bal. Fig.)	160,000	Balance c/d	298,728
	466,728		466,728
	=======		=======

5.3.5 Returns on investments and servicing of finance are receipts resulting from the ownership of investment and payments to providers of finance - the non-equity holders such as the preference shareholders and minority interests (excluding those items required to be classified under other specified headings.) Cash inflows from returns on investments and servicing of finance include: Interest received (together with the related tax recovered), dividends received (net of any tax credits). Cash outflows from returns on investments and servicing of finance include: interest paid (even though it is capitalised) together with any tax deducted and paid to the relevant authority; cash outflows that are treated as finance cost; the interest element of finance lease rental payment; and the dividends paid to non-equity shareholders of the company.

Cash flow from operating activities shown in the reconciliation of operating profit to net cash inflows is usually stated before interest receipts and payments.

For taxation, the cash flows included under this heading are cash flows to or from taxation authorities in relation to the revenue and capital profits of the reporting entity. In practice, this is usually the amount paid for corporation tax.

Value Added Tax (VAT) is not included under this heading. Cash flows should be shown net of any associated VAT unless the tax is irrecoverable. The net movement of the VAT account should normally be allocated to cash flows from operating activities, i.e. it should be treated as part of the normal movement in working capital.

In many statements, there will usually be one figure shown for the corporation tax paid in the year. The preparation of a taxation account detailing all opening and closing tax balances relating to the corporation tax is often the simplest way to derive the tax paid for the year.

5.3.6 Example:

Question: From the extracts of the profit and loss account of DDT Ltd for the year ended 31 December 2011, the following are shown:

	CU	CU
Turnover		XX
Cost of sales		XX
Dividends received		200,000
Profit on ordinary activities before taxation		XX
Taxation:		
Corporation tax		600,000
Deferred Tax		100,000
		700,000
Dividends:		
Interim	192,000	
Final	480,000	
		672,000

Extracts from the company's balance sheet are:

	December 31 2010 CU	2011 CU
Creditors: amount falling due within one year: Corporation tax	340,000	662,000
Provisions for liability and charges: Deferred tax	220,000	260,000

Required:

Calculate the amount of tax paid by DDT Ltd during the year.

Answer:
DDT Ltd – Computation of Tax Paid in the year 2011

Taxation Account

	CU		CU
Tax paid (balancing figure)	338,000	Balance b/d:	
Balance c/d:		Corporation tax	340,000
- Corporation tax	662,000	Deferred tax	220,000
- Deferred tax	260,000	Profit and loss:	
		Corporation tax	600,000
		Deferred tax	100,000
	1,260,000		1,260,000

Note: Information provided here is enough to calculate the tax paid for the year. But it is usually easier to compute tax as a balancing figure. All the tax items are inserted into the tax account and the tax paid automatically follows as the balancing figure on the account.

5.3.7 The cash flows included in the capital expenditure and financial investments are those related to fixed assets, other than those acquired to be classified under acquisition and disposals and any current assets investment not included in the liquid resources.

Cash inflows from capital expenditure and financial investment include:
- Receipts from sales or disposals of property, plant and equipment; and
- Receipts from the repayment of the company's loans to other companies or sales of debt instruments of other companies (not included as part of acquisition or disposal or movement in liquid resources.)

Cash outflows from capital expenditure and financial investment include:
- Payments to acquire property, plant and equipment (including the capital element of the finance lease payments); and
- Loans may by the company and payments to acquire debt instruments of other companies (excluding those forming part of an acquisition or disposal or movement in liquid resources).

5.3.8 Cash flows from acquisitions and disposals relate to the acquisition or disposal of any trade or business, or of an investment in another company. The cash inflows will include:

- Receipts from sales of investment in subsidiary (show separately any balances of cash and overdraft transferred as part of the sale).
- Receipts from sales of investments in associates or joint ventures.
- Receipts from sales of trades or businesses.

Cash outflows will include:
- Payments to acquire investments in subsidiaries;
- Payments to acquire investments in associates and joint ventures;
- Payments to acquire trades or businesses.

5.3.9 The cash flows included in Equity Dividends paid are dividends paid on the company's equity shares. These dividends are reported separately from interest and preference dividends paid to highlight the fact that payment of equity dividends is discretionary.

5.3.10 Liquid resources are current asset investments held for the purpose of trade and disposal. They include such investments that are readily disposable:
• By reporting company without reducing or disrupting business; or
• Are readily convertible into known amounts of cash at or close to its carrying amount; or
• Are traded in an active market.
Short-term deposits, term deposits, government securities, loan stock, equity and derivatives might form part of a company's liquid resources.

Thus, cash inflows in liquid resources would include:
• Withdrawals from short-term deposits (not qualifying as cash in so far as not netted);
• Inflows from disposal or redemption of any other investments held as liquid resources.

Cash outflows would include:
• Payments into short-term deposits (not qualifying as cash in so far as not netted);
• Outflows to acquire any investments held as liquid resources.

Cash inflows and outflows with liquid resources may be netted against each other if they are due to short maturities and high turnover occurring from rollover or reissue, e.g. Short-term deposits.

5.3.11 Financing cash flows consists of receipts or repayments of principal from or to external providers of finance.

Financing cash inflows will include:

- Receipts from issuing of shares or other equity instruments;
- Receipts from issuing of debentures, loan, notes and bonds, and other long-term and short-term borrowings (other than overdrafts.)

Financing cash outflows will include:

- Repayments of amounts borrowed (excluding overdrafts).
- The capital element of finance lease rental payments.
- Payments to reacquire or redeem the company's own shares.
- Payments of expenses or commissions on any issue of equity shares.

5.3.12 Example:
The extracts from the opening and closing balance sheets of TTL Ltd are as follows:

	31.12.2010 CU'000	31.12.2011 CU'000
Creditors: Amount falling due after more than 1year - 10% Convertible unsecured loan stock	868	560
12% Debenture	-	316
Share Capital and Reserves:		
Ordinary Shares of CU1.00 each	300	592
8% Convertible Preference Shares	60	60
Share Premium	156	260

During the year, the following operations took place.
1. CU96,000 of 10% convertible unsecured loan stock was converted into 32,000 ordinary shares; the remaining reduction represents the purchase and cancelation of the loan stock by the company for a total consideration of CU180,000.
2. A bonus issue of one for five shares (in issue at beginning of the year) was made from the share premium.
3. A fresh issue of ordinary shares was made to provide further funds.

Required: Prepare the financing section of the cash flow statement.

Answer.

Note: The conversion of the CU96,000 nominal value of the loan stock into CU32,000 nominal value of the shares means that the premium on the shares is the difference between the two nominal values. The financing section of the cash flow statement will appear as follows:

	CU'000	CU'000
Financing:		
Issue of Debentures	316	
Issue of shares	300	
Purchase of loan stock	(180)	
Net cash inflow from financing		436

Working

	Ord. Share Capital CU'000	Pref. Share Capital CU'000	Share Premium CU'000	Loans CU'000
Balance as at 1 Jan. 2010	300	60	156	868
Conversion of loan stock	32		64	(96)
Issue of Debentures				316
Bonus issue	60		(60)	
Purchase of Loan Stock:				
Consideration –				
-Par Value (868-96-560) = 212				(180)
-Profit on repurchase (212 – 180)				(32)
Share issue (balancing figure)	200		100	
Balance as at 31 December 2010	592	60	260	876

5.3.13 International Financial Reporting Standards 1 (IFRS 1) requires a note reconciling the movement of cash during the period with the movement in net debt (see examples shown earlier on 5.3.2, and 5.3.4). This reconciliation can be given either as part of the cash flow statement or in a note. If the reconciliation is part of the cash flow statement, it should be clearly labelled and kept separate.

The purpose of the reconciliation is to provide information which will

assist in the assessment of liquidity, solvency and financial adaptability.
Net Debt consists of the borrowings of the reporting entity (i.e. the capital instruments classified as liabilities in line with the provisions of IFRS 25 – Financial Instruments: Disclosure and Presentation, together with the related derivatives and obligations under finance leases) **less** cash and liquid resources. Where cash and liquid resources exceed the borrowings of the company, reference should be made to "**Net Funds**" rather than to "**Net Debt**".

To that extent, redeemable preference shares treated as liabilities under IFRS 25 will be included in Net Debt. The definition excludes trade debtors and creditors. While these are short term claims on the sources of finance for the company, their main role is as part of the company's trading activities. Movements in debtors and creditors are dealt with as part of operating activities.

The changes in net debt should be analysed from the opening to the closing component amounts, showing separately, where material, changes resulting from the following:
- The cash flows of the entity
- The acquisition or disposal of subsidiary undertakings
- Other non-cash changes
- The recognition of changes in the market value and exchange rate movements.

5.3.14 Example:
The extract from the opening and closing balance sheets of HOG Ltd are as follows:

	31 December 2010 CU'000	31 December 2011 CU'000
Current assets:		
Investments – in Government stock	236	148
Cash at Bank	80	10
Creditors:		
Amount due falling within 1 year –		
Loan	240	200
Overdraft	-	94
Creditors:		
Amount due falling after more than 1 year		
Loan	200	

(1) The government stock consists of a number of holdings, all of which were made with a view to disposal by the company within three months of acquisition

(2) The loan was originally made in December 2009 with repayments required of CU40,000 every two months.

(3) The overdraft is repayable on demand.

Required:

Show the cash flow for the year ended 31 December 2011, the reconciliation of net cash flow to movement in net debt, and the note analysing movements in net debt.

Answer

HOG Ltd: Cash Flow for the year ended 31 December, 2011

	CU'000
Decrease in cash for the year (80 – 10 + 94)	(164)

Reconciliation of net cash flow to movement in net debt (Note)

Decrease in cash flow during the period	(164)
Cash outflow from decrease in debt	240
Cash inflow from sale of liquid resources (236 – 148)	(88)
Change in net debt	(12)
Net debt at 1 January 2011	(124)
Net debt at 31 December 2011	(136)

Analysis of changes in net debt

	At 1 Jan. 2011 CU'000	Cash Flows CU'000	Other Changes CU'000	At 31 Dec. 2011 CU'000
Cash at Bank	80	(70)		10
Overdrafts	-	(94)		(94)
		(164)		

Debts due within 1 year	(240)	240	(200)	(200)
Debts due after 1 year	(200)		200	-
Current asset investments	236	(88)		148
Total	(124)	(12)	-	(136)

5.3.15 Areas to Note

• Cash flows relating to exceptional items in the profit and loss account should be identified in the cash flow statement or in a note to it, with explanation to the relationship between the cash flows and the originating exceptional item.

• Cash flows relating to provisions for operating items are included in the operating activities, even though the provisions were not included in the profit and loss account. Such examples include redundancy payments falling under a provision for the termination of an operation or for a fundamental reorganisation or restructuring, and operating item cash flows provided for on an acquisition.

• Where cash flows are exceptional, sufficient disclosure should be given to explain their cause and nature.

• Material non-cash transactions should not be reported in a cash flow statement but disclosed separately. Examples of such non-cash transactions include; certain acquisitions and disposals of subsidiaries by a group of companies, finance leases, and certain changes in debt and equity.

• Hire purchase and finance leases are accounted for by the lessee/purchaser capitalising the present value of the minimum lease payments. A liability and a corresponding asset are produced which do not reflect cash flows in the accounting period. IFRS 1 requires a split between the interest and capital elements of the rentals paid on both hire purchase and finance leases – the interest element is shown under servicing of finance, and the capital element is shown under financing. The interest element is calculated and charged to the profit and loss account before taxation. Deducting the interest charge from rentals paid produces the capital paid in the year.

• The non-cash flow elements of a finance lease may need to be disclosed:

1. If the finance lease is of such materiality that it is classified as a major non-cash transaction; and/or
2. in the note reconciling the net cash flow to the movement in net debt as the finance lease liability may have been aggregated with, e.g. bank loans on the balance sheet.

5.3.16 Example:

ABG Ltd entered into a number of finance leases during the current year 2011. There were no such leases in the previous years. Extracts from the balance sheets show the following:

	31 Dec. 2011 CU'000	31 Dec. 2010 CU'000
Fixed Assets:		
Leased property under finance lease	11,420	8,000
Less: Accumulated Depreciation	3,428	2,000
	7,992	6,000
Liabilities:		
Non-current obligations under finance leases	6,502	5,290
Current obligations under finance leases	2,630	2,300
	9,132	7,590

Notes to the accounts – Profit and Loss Account for 2011.

	CU'000
Profit is stated after charging:	
Depreciation of owned assets	4,600
Depreciation of assets held under finance leases	1,428
Finance charges payable:	
Finance leases	1,712
Interest	2,650
Hire of plant and machinery – operating lease	720
Hire of other assets – operating lease	380

Required:

Produce extracts for the cash flow statement as far as information available can.

Answer

ABG Ltd – Extract for the Cash Flow Statement for the year ended 31 December 2011

	CU'000
Returns on investments and servicing of finance:	
- Interest element of finance lease rental	(1,712)
- Interest paid	(2,650)
Financing:	
- Capital element of finance lease rentals (see workings)	(1,878)

Workings:

Grouping the current and non-current obligations together and deriving new finance leases from the increase in fixed asset cost allows the capital element of the rentals to be calculated as the balancing figure.
The operating leases are treated like any other expenses.

Obligations under Finance Leases

	CU'000		CU'000
Capital element of rentals:		Balance b/d:	
- paid during the year	1,878	Current and non-current	7,590
Balance c/d		New finance leases	
Current and non-current	9,132	(from fixed asset increase)	3,420
	11,010		11,010

5.3.17 "Small" Companies Exempted from the provisions of FRS 1

Note that FRS1 - Presentation of Financial Statements – (as amended) does not apply to "small" companies. FRS1 applies to financial statements intended to give a true and fair view of the financial position and profit and loss account excluding those of:

1. Subsidiary undertakings where 90% or more of its voting rights are controlled within the group, as long as the consolidated financial statements in which the subsidiary undertakings are publicly available.

2. Companies incorporated under companies legislation and entitled to the exemptions available in the legislation for small companies when filing accounts with the Registrar of companies.
3. Entities that would have been in class 2 above if they were companies incorporated under companies legislation.
4. Mutual life assurance companies, pension funds, some open-ended investment funds and some building societies.

It is important to understand why FRS 1 exempts subsidiary undertakings where 90% or more of the voting rights in the subsidiary are controlled within the group. It is probable that the liquidity, solvency and financial adaptability of the subsidiary will depend upon the group, rather than on its own cash flows. Usually, groups have centralised cash management operations and cash balances can be moved around the group. In this situation, historical cash flow information of the individual group companies does not always contribute to an assessment of future cash flows.

5.3.18 Advantages of the Cash Flow Statement

Generally, a cash flow statement can provide information which is not available from the balance sheets and profit and loss accounts.
1. It may assist users of financial statements in making judgements on the amount, timing and degree of certainty of future cash flows.
2. It gives an indication of the relationship between profitability and cash generating ability, and thus of the quality of the profit earned.
3. Analysts and other users of financial information most times, formally or informally, develop models to assess and compare the present value of the future cash flows of entities. Historical cash flow information could be used to check the accuracy of past assessments.
4. A cash flow statement in conjunction with a balance sheet provides information on liquidity, viability and adaptability. The balance sheet is usually used to obtain information on liquidity, but the information is incomplete for this purpose as the balance sheet is drawn up at a particular point in time.
5. Cash flow cannot easily be manipulated and it is not affected by subjective judgement or by accounting policies.

5.3.19 Limitations of Cash Flow Statement
In general, cash flow statement is used in combination with the profit and loss account and the balance sheet when making an assessment of the

future cash flows. However:
1. Cash flow statements are based on historical information and therefore do not give complete information for assessing future cash flows.
2. There is a level of manipulation of the cash flows. An instance is where an entity delays paying creditors until after the year end, or it may structure transactions such that the cash balance is favourably affected. Also, an asset may be sold and then immediately repurchased to give favourable position of the cash flows. However, with the provision of the IFRS 5 (Non-current Assets Held for Sale and Discontinued Operations) reporting the Substance of transactions, users of the financial statements will be put on the alert on the true nature of such arrangements.
3. Cash flow is necessary for the survival of any company in the short term, but in order to survive in the long term, a company must be profitable. It is therefore often necessary to sacrifice cash flow in the short run in order to generate profit in the long run, e.g. by investing in fixed assets. A large cash balance is not always a sign of good management if the cash could be invested elsewhere to generate profit.
4. Neither cash flow nor profit provides a complete picture of a company's performance when considered in isolation.

5.3.20 Definition of Cash under FRS

There is a new definition of cash in the revised version of the FRS by the ASB. Here, the ASB decided to use "pure" cash as the basis of the cash flows reported in the cash flow statement. Cash in this case does not include investments or short-term deposits, however liquid or near maturity. The effect of this definition is that the bottom line of the cash flow statement shows the increase or decrease in "pure" cash for the period.

Under the earlier version of the International Accounting Standards - IAS 7 - (Statement of Cash Flows), the cash flow statement showed the movement in cash and cash equivalents. Here, cash equivalents were defined as "short term, highly liquid investments which are readily convertible into known amount of cash without notice and which are within three months of maturity when acquired."

This definition was widely criticised by analysts and preparers of financial statements. Especially, the three months limit was regarded as subjective and arbitrary. Deposits which in practice were used as part of treasury management had to be classified as investments, thus presenting a potentially misleading picture to users of the financial statements.

Thus, in revising the IAS 7, the ASB decided to use pure cash as the basis of cash flows reported in the cash flow statement. In doing so, it also introduced a section for cash flows relating to the management of liquid resources. It believes that the approach has the following advantages:

1. It avoids the arbitrary cut-off point in the definition of the cash equivalents.
2. It distinguishes cash flows arising from accumulating or using liquid resources, from those for other investing activities.
3. It provides information about an entity's treasury activities that were not previously available, to the extent that the instruments dealt in fell within the definition of cash equivalents.

5.3.21 Cash-based/Cash flow accounting ratios

5.3.21a Cash Flow from Operations to Current Liabilities Ratio – This is the financial ratio that shows the liquidity of the business entity by providing a measure of the extent to which current liabilities are covered by cash flowing into the business from normal operating activities. It is given as:

$$\frac{\text{Net cash flow from operating activities}}{\text{Average current liabilities}} \times 100\%$$

5.3.21b Cash Recovery Rate (CRR) – This ratio measures the rate at which a company recovers its investment in fixed assets. The quicker the recovery period obtained, the lower the risk. And this is given as:

$$\frac{\text{Cash Flow from operations}}{\text{Average gross fixed assets}} \times 100\%$$

5.3.21c Cash flow Adequacy Ratio (CFAR) - Measures the ability of the company to operate successfully and stand firm before its financial stability and therefore its credit rating is eroded, and it is given as:

$$\frac{\text{Annual net free cash flow (NFCF)}}{\text{Annual debt repayments and interest}}$$

Where NFCF = Earnings before interest, tax, depreciation and amortisation minus capital expenditure, interest, tax and preference dividends.

5.3.22 Linkages between Financial Statements

There are linkages between the three main financial statements – Balance Sheet, Income Statement, and The Cash Flow Statement. Note the following:

1. The cash and cash equivalents as shown in the balance sheet is a direct product of the cash flow statement which reconciles the cash balances at the beginning and end of the year.
2. Depreciation, as a debit in the Income Statement, for the reporting period is deducted from the tangible fixed assets (e.g. PPE) account to obtain the balance (of PPE) as shown in the Balance Sheet.
3. The Retained Earnings in the Balance Sheet is made up of an addition of the profit for the reporting period as worked out in the Income Statement.

5.3.23 Interpreting Cash Flow Data

For any company, future cash flows are very important. Estimating such is necessary in determining the solvency or otherwise of the company. While financial accounts are historical, they still can provide some evidence of solvency. In interpreting cash flow statements, consideration should be had on: cash generation from the trading activities, dividends and interest payments, capital expenditure and financial investments, management of the liquid resources, and the cash flow.

For the cash generated from operations, the figure should be compared with the operating profit. The reconciliation note to the cash flow statement is useful in this regard. Overtrading may be suggested by: high profits and low cash generation; and large increases in stock, debtors and creditors.

The dividends and interest payments can be compared to the cash generated from the trading activities to determine if normal operations can sustain such payments.

For the capital expenditure and financial investment, note whether the nature and scale of such investment in fixed assets is clearly identified.

The subtotal cash inflow and cash outflow before the use of the liquid resources and financing shows the financing required, unless existing cash is available. The changes in financing, in pure cash terms, are clearly shown. There may be a major non-cash flow changes in the capital structure of the company. The issue of gearing may be considered at this point – all impacting on the management of liquid resources and financing.

The cash flow statement clearly shows the end result in cash terms of the company's activities during the year. However, the importance of this figure should not be overstated. A decrease in the cash during the year may be for a good reason, for instance, the previous year had surplus cash, or may be mainly due to timing difference such as when a new loan is raised just after the end of the accounting period.

In determining the future cash need, other areas of the published financial statements should be considered. Such areas include the need to repay existing loans; requirement to increase the working capital; capital expenditure need; leasing commitments and contingent liabilities.

If there appears to be a cash shortfall, the company may need to take one or more of the following steps to redress the situation:

1. Increase the level of overdraft, if it has not exceeded the limit.
2. Increase its long-term borrowing (taking into account the provisions of its Articles and Memorandum of Association.)
3. Raising cash through issue of shares.
4. Tightening its credit and stock control, and deferring payments to the creditors.
5. Limiting the capital expenditure, or at least postponing them.
6. Entering into sale and leaseback arrangements (with assets which are not already charged.)
7. Selling off some assets or part of assets which will not negatively affect the company.
8. Buying some viable company by issuing its own shares in consideration.

The above measures could be considered in preference to:

9. Reduction of dividend payments; and
10. Reduction in its level of activities.

5.3.24 Unbalanced Financial Development

The growth and development of company activities depend on the availability of a system of forward planning which determines the possible profitability and financial implication of the investment proposals. Though the best-laid plans could be thwarted by an unforeseen circumstance, planning is still relevant to business development; otherwise, the management may embark on projects that will yield unfavourable outcomes even in the most favourable conditions. In practice, management often fail to attain a balanced financial structure, either because it does not plan ahead or because some unexpected events derailed their plans. Unbalanced financial development takes place when management fails to maintain a reasonable level of balance between inflows of resources leading to the deterioration of company financial position. Two possible aspects of unbalanced financial development may be identified, namely: Over-capitalisation and Over-trading.

5.3.25 Over-capitalisation
This occurs when and where management is not able to utilise in full the capital available too it. An example is where the capital structure decided upon fails to achieve the volume of activity anticipated. It could also occur where management finds itself in possession of surplus resources, for instance, following a disposal of some company's activities. Under these circumstances, it may be suggested that a return of capital be made to the stakeholders either by purchasing or redeeming some of its shares or by paying off its debts or reducing capital.

5.3.26 Over-trading
This occurs when the volume of business activity is in excess in relation to the finance provided by the shareholders, with the result that there is over reliance on external finance in the form of loan capital, bank overdraft and trade credit. The condition arises because major errors in the financial policy adopted by management. Often this occurs because management had expanded the volume of business activity beyond the level justified by the resources available to the company. This will invariably lead to insufficiency of funds to meet the current and maturing obligations such as payment of wages, debts due to suppliers, tax payable to the relevant authorities, and overdraft facilities.

Over-trading is a common cause of business failure, and management and their advisers should understand its nature and significance. The financial signs of overtrading which may be apparent in the balance sheet include a decline in the ratios of debtors to creditors, and current assets to current liabilities; a reduced figure for working capital, and even a deficit, a very high ratio of fixed assets to working capital and serious cash shortage.

Part 6

PRACTICE QUESTIONS AND ANSWERS
(on cash flow statements)

Question 1

The summarised balance sheets of BBL PLC at 31 December 2010 and 2011 are as follows:

	2011 CU000	2010 CU000
Freehold property at cost	260,000	220,000
Plant and machinery at cost	302,000	240,000
Fixtures and fittings at cost	58,000	48,000
Stock	102,000	74,000
Debtors	88,000	85,600
Government stock	9,200	-
Cash at bank	22,800	400
	842,000	668,000
Issued Share Capital (Ordinary shares)	300,000	200,000
Share Premium	70,000	30,000
Profit and loss account	72,000	23,000
Debentures	60,000	140,000
Deferred taxation	36,000	22,000
Creditors	96,000	68,000
Bank overdraft	-	28,000
Corporation tax payable	30,000	21,000
Proposed dividends	40,000	20,000
Depreciation on plant and machinery	108,000	90,000
Depreciation on fixtures and fittings	30,000	26,000
	842,000	668,000

Notes:
• There had been no disposal of freehold property in the year.
• A machine tool which cost CU16,000, in respect of which CU12,000 depreciation had been provided, was sold for CU6,000, and fixtures which had cost CU10,000(in respect of which depreciation of CU4,000 had been provided) were sold for CU2,000. Profits and losses on those transactions had been dealt with through the profit and loss account.
• The government stock is a short-term investment traded in an active market.
• The corporation tax liability in respect of the year ended 31 December 2010 amounting to CU21,000 had been paid during the year.
• The profit and loss account charges in respect of tax were: current tax CUU25,000; deferred tax CU19,000.
• The premium paid on redemption of debentures was CU4,000, which has been written off to profit and loss account.
• The proposed dividend for 2010 had been paid during the year.
• Interest received during the year was CU900. Interest charged in the profit and loss account for the year was CU12,800. Accrued interest of CU880 is included in creditors at 31 December 2010 (nil at 31 December 2011.)

Required:
Prepare a cash flow statement for the year ended 31 December 2011, together with notes as required by IAS 7 as amended by the IFRSs.

Suggested Answer 1

BBL PLC: Cash flow statement for the year ended 31 December 2011

Reconciliation of operating profit to net cash flow from operating activities

	CU
Operating profit (Working 7)	150,900
Depreciation charges (Working 5)	38,000
Increase in stocks (102,000 − 74,000)	(28,000)
Increase in debtors (88,000 − 85,600)	(2,400)
Increase in creditors {96,000 − (68,000 − 880)}	28,880
Net cash inflow from operating activities	187,380

Cash Flow Statement

	CU	CU
Net cash inflow from operating activities		187,380
Returns on investments and servicing finance:		
- Interest received	900	
- Interest paid (12,800 – 880)	(13,680)	(12,780)
Taxation: Corporation tax paid (Working 6)		(21,000)
Capital Expenditure:		
- Purchase of tangible assets (Working 2)	(138,000)	
- Receipts from sales of tangible assets	8,000	(130,000)
Equity dividends paid		(20,000)
Net cash outflow before use of liquid resources and financing		3,600
Management of liquid resources:		
- Purchase of government stock		(9,200)
Financing:		
- Issue of share capital (100,000 + 40,000)	140,000	
- Redemption of debentures	(84,000)	56,000
Increase in cash during the period		50,400

Reconciliation of net cash flow to movement in net debt (Note)

Increase in cash during the period	CU 50,400
Cash outflow from redemption of debentures	84,000
Cash outflow from purchase of current asset investment	9,200
Change in net debt resulting from cash flows	143,600
Premium on redemption of debentures	(4,000)
Change in net debt for the period	139,600
Net debt at 1 January 2011	(167,600)
Net debt at 31 December 2011	(28,000)

Note: Analysis of Change in Net Asset

	At Jan. 1 2011 CU	Cash Flows CU	Other Changes CU	At Dec. 31 2011 CU
Cash at bank	400	22,400	-	22,800
Bank Overdraft	(28,000)	28,000	-	-
Debentures	(140,000)	84,000	(4,000)	(60,000)
Current asset investments	-	9,200	-	9,200
Total	(167,600)	143,600	(4,000)	(28,000)

Workings

1.
Plant and machinery Account – at cost

	CU		CU
Balance b/d	240,000	Disposals A/C	16,000
Additions	78,000	Bal. C/D	302,000
	318,000		318,000

2.
Fixtures and Fittings Account – at cost

	CU		CU
Balance b/d	48,000	Disposal a/c	10,000
Additions	20,000	Balance C/D	58,000
	68,000		68,000

Fixed assets – summary of additions

Freehold property	CU40,000
Plant and machinery	78,000
Fixtures and fittings	20,000
	138,000

3.
Plant and machinery account - Depreciation

	CU		CU
Disposal a/c	12,000	Balance b/d	90,000
Balance c/d	108,000	Charge for the year	30,000
	120,000		120,000

4.
Fixtures and Fittings Account – Depreciation

	CU		CU
Disposal a/c	4,000	Balance b/d	26,000
Balance c/d	30,000	Charge for the year	8,000
	34,000		34,000

5.
Fixed Assets Disposals Account

	CU		CU
Plant cost	16,000	Plant depreciation	12,000
Fittings cost	10,000	Fittings depreciation	4,000
Cash proceeds:			
☐ Plant	6,000		
☐ Fittings	2,000		
Depreciation under-			
provided (bal. Figure)	2,000		
	26,000		26,000

Summary of Depreciation

Plant and Machinery	CU30,000
Fixtures and fittings	8,000
Disposals	2,000
	40,000

6.
Taxation
The figure relating to tax that requires computation for the cash flow statement is the total tax paid during the accounting period. To determine that, it is only necessary to enter all opening and closing balances relating to tax and the profit and loss account tax charge into a Tax Account.

Tax Account

	CU		CU
Cash paid (balancing figure)	21,000	Balance b/d:	
Balance c/d:		Deferred tax	22,000
Deferred tax	36,000	Corporation tax	21,000
Corporation tax	30,000	Profit and loss a/c:	
		Deferred tax	19,000
		Corporation tax	25,000
	87,000		87,000

7.
Profit and Loss Account
As the figure for the operating profit is required, you have to reconstruct the profit and loss account up to this figure:

	CU	CU
Operating profit (bal. fig)		150,900
Loss on disposal of fixed assets		(2,000)
Interest received		900
Interest paid		(12,800)
Premium on redemption of debentures		(4,000)
		133,000
Taxation:		
Corporation tax	25,000	
Deferred tax	19,000	(44,000)
		89,000
Dividends		(40,000)
Retained profit for the year		49,000
Balance b/d		23,000
Balance c/d		72,000

Question 2
PWZ PLC has the following information relating to its draft financial statements.

Profit and loss account for the year to 30th June 2011

	CU'000	CU'000
Turnover		7,072
Material consumed	2,158	
Labour costs	1,516	
Production overheads	906	
Cost of sales		(4,580)
Gross profit		2,492
Selling and distribution costs	442	
Administration	504	
		(946)
Interest payable	(170)	
Dividends receivable	48	
		(122)
		1,424
Taxation		(420)
		1,004
Dividends		(700)
Retained profit for the period		304

PWZ PLC Balance sheet as at:

	30 June 2011			30 June 2010		
Fixed assets:	Cost	Depreciation	NBV	Cost	Depreciation	NBV
	CU'000	CU'000	CU'000	CU'000	CU'000	CU'000
Tangible-						
Land and building	4,000	1,500	2,500	3,400	1,490	1,910
Plant and machinery	2,736	1,050	1,686	1,880	620	1,260
	6,736	2,550	4,186	5,280	2,110	3,170

Investments:				
Shares in unquoted Company		1,600		-
		-------		--------
		5,786		3,170
Current assets:				
Stocks	1,516		1,256	
Trade debtors	520		388	
Dividend receivable	30		-	
Bank	44		-	
	--------		--------	
	2,110		1,644	
Creditors: Amounts falling due within one year:				
Trade Creditors	468		506	
Proposed dividends	400		360	
Taxation	502		408	
Government grants	250		150	
Overdraft	-		56	
	-------		-------	
	1,620		1,480	
Net current assets		490		164
Creditors: Amounts falling due after one year:				
Deferred tax	504		282	
Government grants	440		320	
7% Debenture	1,936	(2,880)	-	(602)
	--------	--------	-------	--------
		3,396		2,732
		=====		=====
Share Capital and Reserves:				
Ord. Shares of CU1 each		2,200		2,000
Reserves:				
Share premium	360		200	
Profit and loss A/C	836	1,196	532	732
	-----	--------	-------	--------
		3,396		2,732
		=====		=====

Notes:

1. Included in the turnover are sales of CU1,000,000 to Jato PT Ltd, a company located in Honshu, Japan. The figure consists of two separate sales transactions, both of which have been translated into CU. The first transaction, translated at CU400,000, was paid in Yen, the local currency. PWZ PLC had difficulties in converting the Yen into CU. Jato PT Ltd's main activity relates to the extraction of crude oil, and as a result of previous exchange difficulties, it was agreed that Jato PT Ltd would pay for second transaction in barrels of oil. The spot rate for the crude oil at the date it was shipped to PWZ PLC was CU10 per barrel. PWZ PLC later used the crude oil in one of its manufacturing processes.

2. All depreciation charges and a credit of CU160,000 relating to the amortisation of government grants have been included in production overheads. There were no disposals of fixed assets during the year.

3. During the year, 20,000 ordinary shares were issued to employees under the company's employee share purchase scheme. The market value of these shares was CU100,000. The amount has been correctly recorded in the share capital and share premium. The terms of the share scheme meant that the employees were required to contribute only the nominal value of the shares. The net cost to the company of this transaction has been included in the labour costs.

4. On 1 July 2010, PWZ PLC issued a CU2,000,000 7% Debenture at a discount of 5%. The debenture is redeemable on 30th June 2015 at a premium of 4%. PWZ PLC has amortised the discount and premium on this financial instrument equally (i.e. straight-line) over its five-year life and included the amortisation charge in the interest payable figure.

5. On 1 July 2010, PWZ PLC acquired 15% of the share capital of TTL Ltd, one of its major material suppliers. It has treated this as a fixed asset investment. PWZ PLC has recently received the financial statements of TTL Ltd for the year ended 30th June 2011. These show an interim dividend paid of CU120,000 and proposed final dividend of CU200,000. PWZ PLC received an interim dividend from TTL Ltd in December 2011, and has accrued for its share of the proposed dividend.

Required:

Prepare the Cash Flow Statement for PWZ PLC for the year ended 30th June 2011 (using Direct Method. You are not required to prepare the reconciliation to the operating profit, nor the notes relating to net debt.)

Suggested Answer 2

PWZ PLC: Cash Flow Statement for the Year Ended 30th June 2011

Operation Activities:	CU'000	CU'000
Receipt from customers (Working 1)		6,340
Payments to suppliers (Working 2)		(1,856)
Payments to employees (Working 3)		(1,436)
Other operating expenses (Working 4)		(1,572)
		1,476
Returns on investments and servicing of finance:		
Interest paid (Working 5)	(134)	
Investment income (Working 5)	18	
		(116)
Taxation (Working 6)		(104)
Capital expenditure (Working 7 (1,456 + 1,600 – 380)		(2,676)
		(1,420)
Equity dividends paid (700 + 360 – 400)		(660)
		(2,080)
Financing (Working 8)		2,180)
Increase in cash (44 + 56)		100

Workings (All figures in CU'000)

1. Receipts from customers:

Turnover	7,072
Adjust for debtors (520 – 388)	(132)
Non-cash adjustment – barter transaction	(600)
Cash receipts	6,340

2. Payments to suppliers:

Materials consumed	2,158
Adjust for increase in stock (1,516 − 1,256)	260
Non-cash barter transaction	(600)
Reduction in creditors (506 − 468)	38
	1,856

3. Payments to employees:

Labour costs from question	1,516
Non-cash share issue cost (see Working 8)	(80)
	1,436

4. Other cash operating expenses:

Production overheads	906
Selling and distribution	442
Administration	504
Non-cash items:	
Depreciation (2,550 − 2,110)	(440)
Government grant	160
Cash paid	1,572

5. Returns on investments and servicing of finance:

Interest payable (from question)	170
Amortisation of debenture discount and premium (see below)	(36)
Cash flow for interest cost	134

Dividends from TTL Ltd (interim only = 15% of CU120, 000)	18

The discount on the issue of the debenture is CU100, 000 (5% of CU2, 000,000), and the premium is CU80, 000 (4% of CU2, 000,000). The total of these items (CU180, 000) is being amortised (in straight-line) over five years. Therefore, CU36,000 (CU180,000/5) has been included in interest payable and added to the net proceeds of CU1,900,000 of the debenture to give the balance sheet carrying value of CU1,936,000. The CU36, 000 is not a cash flow and must be adjusted for as shown above.

The cash flow statement should only include dividends actually received (the interim only), the accrual of the proposed final dividend from TTL Ltd is not a cash flow.

6. Taxation:

Charge to profit and loss account	420
Deferred tax (504 – 282)	(222)
Year-end provisions (502 – 408)	(94)
	104

7. Capital expenditure:

Tangible fixed assets:

Cost carried forward	6,736
Cost brought forward	(5,280)
Additions for cash	1,456
Purchase of fixed asset investment	1,600

Government grants:

Balance carried forward (250 + 440)	690
Amortisation in the year	160
Balance brought forward (150 + 320)	(470)
Received in cash during the year	380

8. Financing:

Ordinary shares:

Increase in ordinary share capital (2200 – 2,000)	200
Increase in share premium (360 – 200)	160
Non-cash element – re share purchase scheme (100 – 20)	(80)
Cash received	280

Debentures:

CU2,000,000 issued at 95 (5% discount)	1,900
	2,180

Question 3

The following information is provided for Tiblu Ltd:

Year to 31 December

	2010 CU'000	2011 CU'000
Operating profit after charging depreciation of CU400,000 and crediting profit on the sale of temporary investments of CU840,000	0	1,240
Debtors	562	484
Creditors	632	432
Stocks	350	750

Calculate the cash flow from operating activities of Tiblu Ltd based on the above information, and explain briefly its significance. (4 marks)

Suggested Answer 3

Tiblu Ltd:
Cash flow from operating activities for the year 2011

	CU'000
Operating profit	1,240
Depreciation	400
Profit on sale of temporary investments	(840)
Decrease in debtors (562 – 484)	78
Decrease in creditors (632 – 432)	(200)
Increase in stocks (350 – 750)	(400)
Cash flow from operating activities	278

The above calculation serves to show the quality of the profit figure by disclosing the extent to which it is represented in cash form after making necessary investments or disinvestments in operating working capital. It can be seen, in this case for Tiblu Ltd, that much of the operating profit is due to a non-recurring profit on the sale of temporary investments and that there has been a substantial drain on available cash as a result of the stock increase and the reduced reliance on finance from creditors.

Question 4

The draft 2011 balance sheet of AJALA PLC, together with comparative figures for the previous year, is as follows:

Balance sheet as at 31 December

	2011 CU'000	2010 CU'000
Fixed Assets:		
Tangible asset –		
Plant and machinery	41,340	24,240
Current assets:		
Stocks	10,420	8,350
Debtors and prepayments	6,716	9,824
Cash at bank and in hand	10	2,556
Government securities	520	0
	17,666	20,730
Creditors: Amount falling due within one year –		
Trade creditors and accruals	8,350	4,002
Current corporation tax	2,120	2,422
Proposed dividend	2,000	1,600
Due under finance lease	1,560	1,560
	14,030	9,584
Net current assets	3,636	11,146
Total assets less current liabilities	44,976	35,386
Creditors: Amounts falling due after more than One year –		
Due under finance lease	4,090	5,112
Provision for liabilities and charges –		
Provision for deferred taxation	3,020	2,730
	37,866	27,544

Capital and reserves:
Called up share capital	20,000	16,000
10% preference share capital	1,000	1,000
Share premium account	6,000	-
Profit and loss account	10,866	10,544
	37,866	27,544

The following additional information is provided:

An interim dividend on the ordinary shares of CU1,200,000 was paid on 27 July 2011.

The dividend due in respect of the preference shares is paid on 31 December each year.

The interest element in the lease rental payment made during the year 2011 amounted to CU538,000.

No plant or machinery was sold during the year. Depreciation debited to the profit and loss account amounted to CU7,420,000.

Required:

1. Beginning with the retained profit for 2011, a reconstruction of the profit and loss account of AJALA PLC in order to determine the operating profit for the year.

2. The cash flow statement of AJALA PLC for 2011 prepared in accordance with the requirements of FRS 1. A reconciliation of operating profit to net cash inflow from operating activities should be presented using the indirect method, but other notes to the cash flow statement are not required.

Suggested Answer 4

1. AJALA PLC: Reconstruction of the Profit and Loss Account and Appropriation Account for the year ended 31 December 2011

	CU'000	CU'000
Retained profit for the year 2011:		
(10,866 – 10,544)		322
Dividends: Preference shares	100	
Ordinary – paid	1,200	
-Proposed	2,000	3,300

Profit after taxation		3,622
Taxation charge for the year	2,120	
Transferred to deferred tax account	290	2,410
Profit before taxation		6,032
Interest element of finance lease		538
Operating profit		6,570

2. Cash flow statement for the year ended 31 December 2011

	CU'000	CU'000
Net cash flow from operating activities		19,376
Return on investment and servicing of finance:		
Preference dividend paid	100	
Interest element of finance lease rental payments	538	
		(638)
Taxation paid		(2,422)
Capital expenditure and financial investments:		
Purchase of tangible assets (41,340 – 24,240) + 7,420		(24,520)
Equity dividends paid		(2,800)
Cash out flow before use of liquid resources and financing		(11,004)
Management of liquid resources:		
Purchase of government securities		(520)
Financing:		
Issue of shares		10,000
Capital element of finance lease rental payments		(1,022)
Decrease in cash		2,546

Reconciliation of operating profit to net cash flow from operating activities

	CU'000
Operating profit	6,570
Depreciation charges	7,420
Increase in stocks	(2,070)
Decrease in debtors	3,108
Increase in trade creditors	4,348
Net cash inflow from operating activities	19,376

Question 5

The following information is provided for GTB Ltd relating to its financial affairs:

Profit and loss account for the year ended 31 December, 2011

	CU'000	CU'000
Turnover		1,040
Other cost of goods		(792)
Gross profit		248
Administrative expenses		(96)
Distribution cost		(74)
Operating profit		78
Interest paid		(20)
Profit on ordinary activities before taxation		58
Tax on ordinary activities:		
Charge for the year	(22)	
Transfer to deferred taxation account	(4)	(26)
Profit after taxation		32
Dividends: Preference	(6)	
Ordinary	(12)	(18)
Retained profit for the year		14
Retained profit brought forward		98
Retained profit carried forward		112

Balance sheet as at 31 December

	2011 CU'000	2010 CU'000
Fixed assets at cost	840	580
Less: Accumulated depreciation	206	172
	634	408

Current assets:		
Stocks	398	266
Debtors	246	158
Treasury bills	0	20
Cash and bank balance	0	10
	644	454
Creditors: amounts falling due within one year-		
Trade creditors	196	54
Current corporation tax	22	24
Bank overdraft	264	66
Proposed dividend (including preference, CU3,000)	18	18
	500	162
Net current assets	144	292
Total assets less current liabilities	778	700
Creditors: amount falling due after more than one year –		
Debentures	400	400
	378	300
Provisions for liabilities and charges:		
Provision for deferred taxation	36	32
	342	268
Capital and reserves:		
Called up share capital	140	100
Preference share capital	60	60
Share premium account	30	10
Profit and loss account	112	98
	342	268

The company did not sell any fixed assets during the year. The treasury bills were sold for CU26,000. The profit arising on the sale was included in the turnover figure.

Required:
1. A cash flow statement for GTB Ltd for the year 2011 prepared in accordance with the requirements of FRS 1. A reconciliation of operating profit to net cash inflow from operating activities should be presented using the indirect method, but other notes to the cash flow statement are not required (13 marks)

2. A discussion of the main financial developments during the year 2011.

Suggested Answer 5

GTB Ltd

1. Reconciliation of operating profit to net cash inflow from operating activities

	CU'000
Operating profit	78
Depreciation charges for the year (£206 – 172)	34
Profit on sale of treasury stock (£26 – 20)	(6)
Increase in stock (£398 – 266)	(132)
Increase in debtors (£246 – 158)	(88)
Increase in creditors (£196 – 54)	142
Net cash inflow from operating activities	28

Cash flow Statement for the year ended 31 December 2011

	CU'000	CU'000
Net cash inflow from operating activities		28
Returns on investment and servicing of finance:		
Interest paid	20	
Preference dividend paid	6	(26)
Taxation paid		(24)
Capital Expenditure and financial investment:		
Purchase of tangible fixed assets		(260)
Equity dividends paid		(12)
Cash outflow before use of liquid resources and financing		(294)
Management of liquid resources:		
Sale of treasury bills		26

Financing:
Issue of shares   60

Decrease in cash   (208)
                                                                      ====

2. Discussion will cover the following areas:
Most of the resources generated from trading in the form of profit before depreciation has been absorbed in the net increase in the working capital. The net cash flow from operating activities, of CU28,000 is insufficient to cover interest payments, tax and dividends which together totalled CU62,000.

The company has undertaken a major investment in fixed assets suggesting an increase in capacity of about 50%; the increase in stocks and debtors represent further evidence of material increase in the scale of operations.

Some of the finance for these developments has been provided from long term sources in the form of share issue. Moreover, the company has sold its holding in treasury bills. GTB Ltd has raised insufficient long-term finance to fund its development with the result that the bank overdraft has increased by about 300% and the increase in the trade creditors is outmatched the apparent rise in the level of operations. The company's net assets are drastically reduced and this is indicative of a financial difficulty facing it.

Question 6

OCS Ltd is a well-established company. Its summarised financial statements for the year to 31 December 2011, together with the comparative figures for the year 2010, contained the following details:

Profit and loss account for the year ended 31 December

	2011	2010
	CU'000	CU'000
Turnover	60,750	40,500
Operating profit	4,248	2,026
Interest paid	1,080	-

	2011	2010
Profit on ordinary activities before taxation	3,168	2,026
Tax on profit on ordinary activities	792	694
Profit after taxation	2.376	1,332
Ordinary dividends proposed	1,350	900
Retained profit for the year	1,026	432
Retained profit brought forward	7,992	7,560
Retained profit carried forward	9,018	7,992

Balance Sheet as at 31 December

	2011 CU'000	2010 CU'000
Tangible fixed assets at cost	27,000	18,000
Less: Accumulated depreciation	9,900	7,200
	17,100	10,800
Intangible fixed assets at cost:		
Development cost	900	1,350
Current assets:		
Stocks	3,960	2,700
Trade debtors	10,468	5,400
Cast at bank and in hand	0	316
	14,428	8,416
Creditors: amounts falling due within one year –		
Trade creditors	2,944	1,980
Bank overdraft	2,124	-
10% Debentures	1,800	-
Current corporation tax	792	694
Proposed dividends	1,350	900
	9,010	3,574
Net current assets (liabilities)	5,418	4,842
Total assets less current liabilities	23,418	16,992

Creditors: amount falling due after more than a year		
10% Debentures	5,400	-
	18,018	16,992
	=====	=====
Capital and reserves:		
Called-up share capital	6,000	6,000
Share premium account	3,000	3,000
Profit and loss account	9,018	7,992
	18,018	16,992
	=====	=====

The following further information is provided:

1. A major advertising campaign was undertaken during the month of December 2010 at a cost of CU1,340,000, and 50% increase in sales was achieved with effect from 1 January 2011. The Directors of OCS Ltd have decided to amortise the development expenditure equally over a three-year period.
2. Fixed assets costing CU9,000,000 were purchased on 1 January 2011 and became fully operational on that date.
3. The debentures are repayable at the of CU1,800,000 per annum with the first repayment due on 1 January 2012.
4. The acquisition of the new fixed assets was partly financed out of bank overdraft facility of CU3,000,000 available for a two-year period ended 31 December 2012.
5. It has been estimated that during the next three years the only material capital expenditure will be to replace a fully depreciated asset in October 2012 as a cost of CU860,000.
6. The levels of stocks, debtors and creditors are not expected to alter materially during the year 2012.
7. It is expected that the turnover and operating profit for the year to 31 December 2011 will be repeated over the following twelve months.

Required:
1. Prepare a cash flow statement for GTB Ltd for the year 2010, prepared in accordance with the requirements of FRS 1. A reconciliation of operating profit to net cash inflow from operating activities should be presented using the indirect method, but other notes to the cash flow statement are not required (6 marks)

2. Calculate the following accounting ratios for each year:
(a) Current ratio
(b) Rate of collection of debtors
(c) Operating profit percentage
(d) Fixed assets turnover
(e) Post-tax return on shareholders' equity. (4 marks)

3. Prepare a report on the financial progress, financial position and prospect of GTB Ltd based on the information given in the question and the results of your calculations under (1) and (2). Prepare an estimated cash flow statement of the year ended 31 December 2012 to show whether it will be possible for the company to achieve repayment of the bank overdraft by the end of the year 2012. (10 marks)

Note: Assume a 365-day year for the purpose of your calculations; calculations to the nearest one decimal place; make and state any assumptions you consider appropriate.

Suggested Answer 6

1.
OCS Ltd: Cash flow statement for the year ended 2010

	CU'000
Net cash flows from operating activities	2,034
Returns on investment and servicing of finance:	
Interest paid	(1,080)
Taxation paid	(694)
Capital expenditure and financial investment:	
Purchase of tangible fixed assets	(9,000)
Equity dividend paid	(900)
Cash outflow before use of liquid resources and financing	(9,640)
Financing:	
Issue of debentures	7,200
Increase/(Decrease) in cash	(2,440)

Reconciliation of operating profit to net cash inflow from operating activities:

	CU'000
Operating profit	4,248
Depreciation charge on tangible fixed assets	2,700
Amortisation of development expenditure	450
Increase in stock (3,960 – 2,700)	(1,260)
Increase in trade debtors (10,468 – 5,400)	(5,068)
Increase in trade creditors (2,944 – 1,980)	964
Net cash inflow from operating activities	2,034

2.

Ratio **Calculation**

		2011	2010
Current ratio:	14,428 : 9,010	1.6 : 1	
	8,416 : 3,574		2.4 : 1
Rate of debtors collection:			
	10,468/60,750 x 365 days	63 days	
	5,400/40,500 x 365 days		49 days
Fixed Assets turnover:	60,750 : 18,000	3.4 : 1	
	40,500 : 12,150		3.3 : 1
Operating profit percentage:			
	4,248/60,750 x 100%	7%	
	2,026/40,500 x 100%		5%
Post-tax return on Shareholders' equity:			
	2,376/18,018 x 100%	13.2%	
	1,332/16,992 x 100%		7.8%

3.
Cash flow Statement for the year ended 31 December 2012

	CU'000
Net cash flows from operating activities	7,398
Returns on investment and servicing of finance:	
Interest paid (assumed)	(1,080)
Taxation paid	(792)
Capital expenditure and financial investment:	
Purchase of tangible fixed assets	(860)
Equity dividends paid	(1,350)
Cash inflow before use of liquid resources and financing	3,316
Financing:	
Repayment of debentures	(1,800)
Increase/(Decrease) in cash	15,16

Reconciliation of operating profit to net cash inflow from operating activities

Operating profit	4,248
Depreciation charge on tangible fixed assets	2,700
Amortisation of development expenditure	450
Net cash inflow from operating activities	7,398

Financial progress and position

- A large proportion of the cash generated from operations during the year 2011 was used to fund a major increase in debtors leaving a balance of CU2,034,000 to meet other expenditure during the year.
- The entire net cash flow from operating activities was absorbed in the payment of interest, dividends and taxation. Indeed, the outgoings exceeded inflows by CU640,000.
- The major capital expenditure programme during the year 2010 was funded 80% through debentures (CU7,200,000) with the balance provided by bank overdraft facilities.
- The overall result was that the cash balance during the year declined by CU2,440,000.

- The effect of the financing arrangements of the new fixed assets was responsible for the reduction in the current ratio from 2.4 : 1 to 1.6 : 1. This is not necessarily a cause for concern as there still remains a good margin between current assets and current liabilities.
- The advertising campaign at the end of 2010 appears to have been entirely successful in producing an expected increase in turnover of 50% during the year 2011.
- A major problem has been the substantial increase in the rate of collection of debtors from 49 days to 63 days. Had the 49-day repayment period been retained, then the debtors at the end of 2011 would have been in the region of CU8,156,000.
- The extension of the collection period has therefore resulted in an increases investment in debtors of CU2,330,000. Every effort should be made to reduce the collection period and thus increase the cash balance accordingly.
- Another concern is the collectability of the full amount of the debtor balances in view of the increasing figure of the amounts outstanding.
- The significant increase in capacity obtained by the fixed assets acquisition appears to have been fully utilised, with the fixed asset turnover ratio more favourable for 2011; 3.4:1 compared with 2010, 3.3:1
- The profit percentages have also increased during 2011, with the operating margin increasing from 5% to 7% and the post-tax return on shareholders' equity up from 7.8% to 13.3%

Financing Prospects
- Given the expectation of no increase in investment in the working capital, the company can expect an impressive net cash inflow from operating activities during the year 2012 of CU7,398,000.
- There will be outflows for interest, taxation and dividends and there is also a planned purchase of fixed assets of CU860,000. However, after meeting these costs, the company will produce a cash inflow before financing of CU3,316,000.
- The company will of course have to meet a repayment of debentures of CU1,800,000 during the year 2012 and this will leave available CU1,516,000 to go towards the repayment of the bank overdraft.
- Assuming these forecasts are fulfilled, the company will be unable to meet the bank's requirement to repay the overdraft by the end of 2012, with an outstanding deficit of CU608,000 (CU2,124,000 – 1,516,000) remaining. The directors will therefore need to approach the bank for a renewal of the overdraft facility or arrange alternative funding.
- It must be noted that the next debenture repayment of CU1,800,000 will fall due on 1 January 2013.

Part 7

IFRS for SMEs – An Illustrative Example of a set of Consolidated Financial Statements

(a) Consolidated Statement of Financial Position
(b) Consolidated Statement of Comprehensive Income – by nature of expense
(c) Consolidated Statement of Changes in Equity
(d) Consolidated Statement of Cash Flows

The IASB developed the IFRS for SMEs in recognition of the difficulty and cost to private companies of preparing fully compliant IFRS information. It also recognised that users of private entity financial statements have different focus from those interested in publicly quoted companies. This standard attempts to meet the users' needs while balancing the costs and benefits to preparers.

This example is designed for information. While effort has been made to be as accurate and comprehensive as possible, the details contained may not cover all the aspects of the standard – some information may have been omitted that may be relevant to a particular user; it is therefore not intended as a substitute for reading the actual standards and interpretations when dealing with specific issues.

The example provides, for illustrative purposes, a set of consolidated financial statements, prepared in line with the provisions of IFRS for SMEs for an assumed agricultural produce company, wholesale and retail group, XYZ Limited.

This example shows how IFRS for SMEs could be applied to a company that has many different types of assets and business arrangements. In the real world, few companies using the IFRS for SMEs will be as complex as this. Certain items may not apply to some entities. For instance, if the entity does not have material operating leases, disclosure of the accounting policy for operating leases does not need to be included.

In this illustrative example, the following assumptions were made:
(a) The entity does not fulfill the requirements for presenting a combined statement of income and retained earnings. Instead, it presents a consolidated statement of comprehensive income and a consolidated

statement of changes in equity (as stated under Section 3 paragraph 18 of IFRS for SMEs).
(b) The entity is a first-time adopter of IFRS for SMEs.
(c) The entity has complex transactions such as business combinations, discontinued operations, share-based payments, government grants, hedge accounting and biological assets.
(d) XYZ Limited owns 100% of the voting rights in all of its subsidiaries.

Certain accounting policy choices have been made in preparing the financial statements, for example, the application of fair value for investment property and biological assets. Certain types of transaction have been excluded, as they are not relevant to the group's operations.

This sample disclosure is not to be considered the only acceptable form of presentation. The form and content of each reporting entity's financial statements are the responsibility of the entity's management.
Some countries may require separate statements to be published for the parent company in addition to consolidated financial statements as is the case in Europe based on the European Union Directives. Here, we have assumed that XYZ Limited is not required to prepare separate financial statements.
The references in the financial statements represent the paragraph of the standard in which the disclosure appears. For instance, "25p4" shows IFRS for SMEs Section 25, Paragraph 4. The actual words and figures for the "Note" are not shown here, but the "numbers" are shown to reflect the requirement of the Standard.

XYZ Limited
Consolidated Financial Statements
31 December, 2011

Contents
(a) Consolidated Statement of Financial Position
(b) Consolidated Statement of Comprehensive Income – by nature of expense
(c) Consolidated Statement of Changes in Equity
(d) Consolidated Statement of Cash Flows

(Note: All amount in thousands in the presentation currency (CU) of the financial statements, unless otherwise stated.)

(a) **Consolidated Statement of Financial Position**
As at 31 December (4p2, 4p9, 4p10)

	Note	2011	2010
Assets			
Current Assets (4p5)			
Cash and Cash Equivalents	5	4,256	6,814
Derivative Financial Instruments	7	292	240
Trade and other Receivables	8	4,418	3,936
Inventories	9	4,940	3,636
Biological Assets	10	346	0
		14,252	14,626
Non-Current Asset (4p6)			
Property, Plant and Equipment	11	31,068	20,046
Investment Property	12	2,364	1,594
Intangible assets	13	5,254	4,140
Biological Assets	10	3,484	2,982
Investments in Associates		2,674	2,648
Deferred Income Tax Assets	26	704	664
		45,548	32,074
Total Assets		59,800	46,700
Liabilities (4p4, 4p7)			
Current Liabilities			
Borrowing	14	2,344	3,652
Trade and other Payables	15	3,334	2,496
Current Tax Liability		514	554
Provisions	16	536	602
Total Current Liabilities		6,728	7,304
Non-Current Liabilities (4p8)			
Borrowings	14	23,024	19,270
Deferred Tax Liability	26	2,474	1,810
Employee Benefit Obligations	17	928	446
Provisions	16	292	80
Total Non-Current Liabilities		26,718	21,606
Total Liabilities		33,446	28,910
Equity	18	26,354	17,790
Total Equity attributable to the owners of the parent		26,354	17,790
Total Liabilities and Equity		59,800	46,700

(b) **Consolidated Statement of Comprehensive Income – by nature of expense**
(Note: 5p11 also allows a classification of expenses by function, whichever provides information that is reliable)

	Note	Year Ended 31 December {5p2(a), 5p4, 5p5} 2011	2010
Revenue {5p5 (a)}	20	38,652	20,916
Other Income	21	3,934	2,156
Change in inventories of finished goods and W.I.P	9	(1,390)	460
Raw Materials and Consumables used		(10,164)	(6,544)
Gain/(loss) arising from changes in fair value of Biological Assets	10	(924)	82
Gain/(loss) from changes in fair value of Investment Property	12	770	(174)
Employee salaries and benefit expense	22	(8,016)	(3,098)
Depreciation and Amortisation	11/13	(4,206)	(2,370)
Transportation expense		(1,916)	(1,248)
Advertising Costs		(2,190)	(700)
Research and Development		(1,162)	(390)
Operating lease expenses{20p16(b)}		(2,120)	(1,700)
Other gains/(losses) – Net	23	(20)	14
Other expenses	24	(356)	(170)
Operating Profit		**10,892**	**7,234**
Finance Income	25	346	322
Finance Costs {5p5(b)}	25	(1,668)	(2,410)
Finance Cost – Net		**(1,322)**	**(2,088)**
Profit before Income Tax		9,570	5,146
Income Tax Expense {5p5(d)}	26	(2,922)	(1,736)
Profit for the year from continuing operations		6,648	3,410
Discontinued Operations:			
Profit for the year from discontinued operations {5p5(e)}	27	20	26
Profit for the year {5p5(f)}		**6,668**	**3,436**
Other Comprehensive Income {5p5(g)}			
Gains/(losses) recognised directly in Equity {5p4(b)}			
Currency transaction differences		1,588	(32)

Actuarial loss on employee benefit obligations, net of tax		0	(98)
Changes in fair value of hedging instruments, net of tax		38	74
Transfer to foreign exchange gains/(losses)		(58)	0
Other Comprehensive Income for the Year, net of tax		1,568	(56)
Total Comprehensive Income for the Year {5p5(i)}		**8,236**	**3,380**
Profit attributable to: Owners of the Parent Company (5p6)		6,668	3,436
Total Comprehensive Income attributable to: Owners of the Parent Company		**8,236**	**3,380**

(c) **Consolidated Statement of Changes in Equity Attributable to Owners of the Parent Company**

	Share Capital and Share Premium (note 18	Other Reserves	Retained Earnings	Total
At January 2010	6,084	1,272	9,694	17,050
Profit for the year			3,436	3,436
Currency translation differences		(32)		(32)
Actuarial loss on employee benefit Obligations, net of tax		(98)		(98)
Changes in fair value of hedging Instruments, net of tax		74		74
Total Comprehensive Income for the year		**(56)**	**3,436**	**3,380**
Operating Profit plus Comprehensive Income		1,216	13,130	20,430
Dividend paid			(3,394)	(3,394)
Employee share option schemes				
- Value of employee services		186		186
- Issue of shares	568			568
At 31 December 2010	**6,652**	**1,402**	**9,736**	**17,790**
Profit for the year	-	-	6,668	6,668
Currency translation differences	-	1,588	-	1,588

Changes in fair value of hedging Instruments, net of tax	-	38	-	38
Transfer to foreign exchange Gain/(losses)		(58)	-	(58)
Total comprehensive income for the year	-	1,568	6,668	8,236
Employee share option schemes				
- Value of employee services	-	138	-	138
- Issue of shares	190	-	-	190
At 31 December 2010	**6,842**	**3,108**	**16,404**	**26,354**

(d) Consolidated Statement of Cash Flows

	Note	Year ended 31 December 2011	2010
Cash Flows from operating activities			
Profit including discontinued operations		6,668	3,436
Adjustments for non-cash income and expenses:			
- Taxes	26	2,922	1,736
- Depreciation	11	3,554	1,932
- Amortisation	13	652	438
- Impairment of trade receivables	8	96	70
- Reduction in provision for impairment of inventories	16	146	(98)
- Fair value (Gains)/Losses – Biological assets	10	924	(278)
- Fair value (Gains)/Losses – Investment property	12	(770)	(174)
- (Profit)/Loss on disposal of property, PPE	23	(4)	20
- Share-based payment and increase in retirement Benefit obligations		306	218
- Fair value (gains)/Losses on hedging instruments	23	54	(42)
- Finance costs – net	25	1,322	2,088
- Unrealised foreign exchange losses/(gains) on Operating activities		(356)	(306)

- Changes in working capital (excluding the effects of acquisition and exchange differences on Consolidation:			
- Trade and other receivables	8	(578)	(746)
- Inventories	9	(1,304)	(902)
- Trade and other payables	15	(798)	(590)
Cash generated from operations		10,738	6,802
Interest paid	25	(2,174)	(2,656)
Income tax paid		(1,548)	(1,126)
Net Cash from operating activities		**7,016**	**3,020**
Cash Flows from investing activities			
Acquisition of subsidiary, net cash acquired	30	(2,790)	0
Purchases of PPE	11	(1,952)	(1,208)
Proceeds from sale of PPE		1,378	634
Purchases of biological assets	10	(1,232)	(214)
Purchases of intangible assets	13	(1,034)	0
Interest received	25	192	196
Dividends received		0	0
Net Cash used in investing activities		**(5,438)**	**(592)**
Cash flows from financing activities			
Proceeds from issuance of ordinary shares		190	568
Proceeds from borrowings		4,012	2,414
Repayments of borrowings		(1,084)	0
Dividends paid to company's shareholders		0	(3,394)
Net Cash used in Financing Activities		**(3,482)**	**(412)**
Net (decrease)/increase in cash, cash equivalents and Bank overdrafts		(1,904)	2,016
Cash, cash equivalents and bank overdrafts at Beginning of the year		5,522	3,518
Exchange gains/(losses) on cash, cash equivalents And bank overdrafts		108	(12)
Cash, cash equivalents and bank overdrafts at End of the year	5	**3,726**	**5,522**

www.ingramcontent.com/pod-product-compliance
Lightning Source LLC
Chambersburg PA
CBHW030933180526
45163CB00002B/548